The Long Poems of Robert Kroetsch Completed Field Notes

The Long Poems of Robert Kroetsch

COMPLETED

ROBERT KROETSCH

FIELD NOTES

The University of Alberta Press

Published by
The University of Alberta Press
Ring House 2
Edmonton, Alberta   T6G 2E1

Printed in Canada   5   4   3   2   1
Text copyright © Robert Kroetsch 1989, 2000
Introduction copyright © Fred Wah 2000
A volume in (*cuRRents*), an interdisciplinary series. Jonathan Hart, series editor.

CANADIAN CATALOGUING IN PUBLICATION DATA

Kroetsch, Robert, 1927–
    Completed field notes

    ISBN 0–88864–350–0

    I. Title.
PS8521.R7C65 2000   C811'.54   C00–910504–2
PR9199.3.K7C65 2000

All rights reserved.

No part of this publication may be produced, stored in a retrieval system, or transmitted in any form or by any means, electronic, mechanical, photocopying, recording, or otherwise, without the prior permission of the copyright owner.

Printed and bound in Canada by Houghton Boston, Saskatoon, Saskatchewan.
∞ Printed on acid-free paper.

The University of Alberta Press gratefully acknowledges the support received for its program from the Canada Council for the Arts. The Press also acknowledges the financial support of the Government of Canada through the Book Publishing Industry Development Program for its publishing activities.

Always, for Megan and Laura

"Before meeting you I was vainly trying to finish a long poem."
—Hubert Aquin, *Prochain Episode*

Contents

Field 1: Robert Kroetsch once told me that he starts writing a novel not from the beginning or from the end, but from somewhere in the middle. That is, he writes his novels from the inside out. I was surprised, since I've always thought of novels as having more to do with endings. As readers of his novels, we really don't need to know this. We begin at a beginning and listen, page after page, for the conclusion, some closure of the narrative. A shot cracks over the lake; the osprey flies up, startled from its nest on the pilings; the end. He's never told me how he writes a poem, but I would guess, from reading his poems, that he begins in the middle there as well. The difference is, his poems are more about staying in that middle. We begin, again, at a beginning, but the poem soon entangles its reading in a process that refuses closure.

Field 2: Kroetsch's poetry is full of information about its presence: how the poem begins, how it works, and, with great insistence, how the poem tries not to end. But even then, as the poem seeks awareness of its own making, we find only the impossibility of either beginnings or endings. As a reader of poems, I trust that I can begin at the beginning, as in the novel, top left to bottom right. There the similarity to the linear progression of the novel ends. In the poem's territory I recognize very quickly that I am caught in what seems more like the middle of something, a labyrinth of possibility, questions that claim they are answers, hyphenated gestures and impersonations, out of which chance meanings reveal themselves.

Field 3: In the poem, it seems, Kroetsch is eager to expose the condition of the poem's composition. We begin within a large space, indeterminate, setting out in the dark, so to speak. The "Grand Design" of the novel seems distant. We are occupied in an activity that has less to do with destination than with being. "Mile Zero" begins with this useful epigraph:

> ...hockey is a *transition game;* offence to defence, defence to offence, one team to another. Hundreds of tiny fragments of action, some leading somewhere, most going nowhere. Only one thing is clear. Grand designs don't work.
> —KEN DRYDEN, *The Game*

Kroetsch's poem, in other words, attempts to avoid design, to occupy a position of unresolved transition. The poem as field becomes a translucent white surface of trajectory, a field of particles that, above all else, seeks constant motion and resists rest. The advantage of such a poetics of process is epistemological. The grand design of the poem, that oppressive authority of the speaking and spoken "I" of the normative lyric poem can be intervened, subverted. "Mile Zero," for example, undercuts the intended control of that poetic voice by removing lines from a stanza

> partly because the sexual innuendo puts me, as actual poet behind the implied speaker ("I") in a bad light; that is, self-mockery is, so to speak, harder to come by, as one (the poet, the implied speaker, the I of the "I") grows older (RK).

Poet and reader straddle the blue line, one jump ahead or behind, inside but offside. Slap shot, slap stick. Overtime.

Notes 1: But our desire (and habit) to make meaning from the fragments, to see pattern and connection, creates another hunger, a necessary propulsion for movement. If our reading is not directed by the need for completion, we must syncretize dissonance, seemingly unconnected particles "going nowhere," in order, by chance, to intersect with a present moment that leads, perhaps, somewhere. And that present moment, given the phenomenological status of Kroetsch's poetics, seems to be the action of the writing itself. The poem is its own writing, the poem as the place of what is.

Field 4: Kroetsch manages this state of apprehension, surely, out of his experience in the novel. He is deft at using the devices of narrative to provide the tension needed to move, not forward but around, in the poem. The spoken subject, that named speaking "I" in the poem, seems always on a slippery and sliding scale between storyteller and poet. The speaking subject in the poems is not that referee of grand designs, the lyric poet. The story-seeker-teller is present to make sure of that. The voice in these fields of interrogation, rather, speaks from a position of between-ness, seemingly caught in a middle that generates constant mediation and continuous motion. As he says in "Mile Zero," "the story of the poem/become/the poem of the story."

Notes 2: But even when Kroetsch tells us, as he does in "Stone Hammer Poem," that the poem began with the stone hammer paperweight on his desk, we cannot be sure he really knows.

> ?what happened
> I have to/I want
> to know (not know)
> ?WHAT HAPPENED

Is this ambivalence just unpredictable stickhandling or an example of "The book that lies permanently" ("The Ledger")? It's not just a question of "?WHAT HAPPENED," but what's happening. The poem seems determined to dwell in and on the implied hyphen between "to know" and "(not know)." This is a stasis that holds us to the moment of composition as a fact, a truth, not a consequence. As the American poet Robert Duncan once said, "You tell the truth the way the words lie."

Notes 3: One way to hold the moment of composition's attention is to keep asking questions, stall for more time, pose mystery, doubt, uncertainty. How do you grow a gardener, a lover, a prairie town, a past, a poet, "Seed Catalogue" asks. That phony Sad Phoenician and-ing and but-ing philosophically as Zeno, Pythagoras, or Lao Tzu between Swift Current and Nanaimo ends up as an editorial (and Swiftian?) query,

"Who?him," a not-so-silent silent poet who, among other things, "Eats his words." "What can we say for certain?" begins "Delphi: Commentary." Even the Oracle's answer is a question:

I was surprised at my own answer when my daughters asked me what I had asked. They knew I had fallen behind to get on with my listening. Or should I say, my questioning? They, somehow, knew that. I was surprised when I offered my explanation. I didn't have a chance, I said. My father asked the question first.

> What are you doing here?
> My father said.
> Did I teach you nothing?

Think of "field notes" as temporary, as momentary gestures that interpolate possibility. Perhaps even as investigations into the potential for narrative. Or at least the poem's capacity for narrative. Then think of narrative not as a predictable line of action and consequence but as a maze of sudden twists, obstacles, impossibilities, possibilities. Kroetsch's *Field Notes* are not only lessons in the naïveté of completion, lessons, in fact, on being lost, they are also a manual of field note technique. The cataloguing of seeds becomes a register of questions about how to grow a poet; the sad Phoenician's alphabet crumbles into the silence of static bounced between conjunctions; the journal of time is erased by its own writing.

Notes 4: In the early 1980s bpNichol and Frank Davey solicited responses from poets to questions of "notation." Several volumes of *Open Letter* documented the variety of replies. "The Frankfurt *Hauptbahnhof*" is Kroetsch's engagement with this project. Notation, as much as we may take it for granted, is constructed in the service of meaning. The poem is not merely a story broken up into lines ("or so the story goes"). If notation, in *Field Notes*, is to be considered beyond its inherited transparent temporal function, then in order to explore its function as a site of intersecting possibilities it must be seen, phenomenally, as part of the Taoist-like process of that which exists through itself: "notation is / (what is..."

Notes 5 / Field 5: "The Frankfurt *Hauptbahnhof*" is a poem about being lost. "couldn't find the train ... couldn't ... couldn't find." "I expected to find ..." but instead "I found ..." "I couldn't see ... I couldn't read ... I was close to despair ... I couldn't find the train, I couldn't catch the train..." Then, a stranger, a "Double or / noting. / My / *doppelgänger*." The notation for being found is the same as for being lost, a double.

Notation is the double of the poem. Or: we are the poem, and cannot hear except by indirection. We can only guess the poem by encountering (by being surprised by) its double. The notation announces the poem to the poem. Perhaps every poem is a poem lost (in the poet, in the reader), and can only find itself in the

broken
(the remaining)
lines.

The field is there to be noted. "The voice" [of the other] "had been exactly my own."

Field 6: "The notation" of "the mysterious text" is what "keeps [the poem] moving." The "Delphi" poem is central to this collection and to late twentieth-century Canadian poetry for its sensitive attention to the discernment of its own movement. As a poetic journal it documents not only a day trip of the poet and his daughters to Delphi but it registers, also, one of the clearest records of contemporary poetic practice. It is, as are many of the poems in this book, about the imagination of place. And space. It is through poems like "Seed Catalogue," "The Sad Phoenician," "Mile Zero," and "Delphi: Commentary" that we can witness those invisible manoeuvres of our imagination over such large space, prairie space, sea-to-shining-sea space, frozen norths and frozen rinks, vastness. Imagine. Space with enough time to be lost.

Field 7: But the "Delphi" poem comes down to a stone cup-hole, the navel of the western world on the side of a mountain in a small village in a small country. What the poem brings to this point, this climactic juncture of western civilization, is a shapeliness of poetic attention that reveals also the expansiveness of poetic space. The shapeliness can be seen, literally, on the page: the letter S in reverse; the E of eggplant juxtaposing a run-around text of history, journal, and poetic horseplay; the shapes of white space between citations, description, reflections that dimly outline broken and possible glyphs. The spaces of the poem, delineated and etched by fragment, quotation, and reportage, tempt us with the illusion of order and progression, "a question, seeking / a speaker."

Field 8: Seemingly, entering this poem places us within an orderly sequence of events: a guided tour on the road to Delphi. The speaker sought by the question listens parenthetically to the loudspeaker on the bus. Then, just as parenthetically, the "[abandoned] / poem / speaks." But what it speaks is "silence." The sureness of order is continually undermined by paradox and contradiction; the ruins of Greece (and of the poem) are, despite the contemporary Pausanian tour, "a labyrinth without a clue, a riddle without an answer." The poem is always that way, we are told, and all it can do is evade itself.

Field 9: This is not a conventionally inhabited space, transparent in its assumed definition of itself, but, rather, an "[abandoned]" poem that in its abandonment is a conversation about a poem, itself and many other poems, about how the poem as answer is also the poem as question. "That's the way it is." The poem is constantly face to face with its own impossibility. Abandon hope for an easy way out. Be lost!

Field 10 / *Completed* 1: A poem as field, like any other space, is not neutral. It is not merely a locator within a cultural guidebook, a signpost truth pointing always the right way. Like any space, the poem has a history of intentions distilled by change and desire into some measure of possibility. The normative lyric poem posits, we expect, a safe and static truth, a site filled with beautiful answers. The poems in this collection register the shifting (and shifty) location of a different kind of poem, one in which boundaries or margins coalesce into middle distances of opposition and contrast. "Every year is the same: / it's different." As for Penelope, the story, in the poem, is to be given to ourselves, not to others. Poetry, here, is in an unlocatable space, lost in space:

> By meaning we mean something that means
> but, in the process, means its opposite.
> We write books to avoid
> writing books.

Completed 2: The conundrum of collecting together a series of poems purported to abhor closure into a "Completed" project is answered only by the author's note that the sequence is "in its acceptance of its own impossibilities, completed." These poems are to "stand," we are told, "as the enunciation of ... a poet's silence." Silence becomes the answer to the question that drives these poems, "How do you...?"

Completed 3 / *Notes* 6: The "advice" in "Advice to My Friends" poses the cadence, the *cadenza*, as the unit of composition where such silences can be observed and noted. At the end of the day, the "sigh, the day's task/accomplished." The open silence of the question that confuses completion:

> What would happen if, just as you
> slid into home plate,
> the pitcher threw the catcher
> an orange?

Or the "storm: you say it's over now," but you're "seasick." A good "gift" at a wedding is "an escape plan." "If you eat the berries ... the pail will never fill." Cadence, in Kroetsch's poetry, pretends to the possibility of ending while noting how not to.

Completed 4: I waited all winter for the new poems; he told me, he would add to what had earlier been complete. I waited for these additions to the edition. He intended to include them, he told me when we met in the folds of the foothills last fall. I believed him, but they never showed up. Has he out-faked my own grand designs for his book? What comes after the last poem in this book, "After Paradise," is (finally?) more silence, the newly silenced poems I waited for. They have become rumours and cul-de-sacs. Wasn't that one of the new ones I heard at his reading? What about the limited edition chapbook you can only find on an island? Is the ongoing hush a clue?

Notes 7: "I didn't mean to change. But he did."

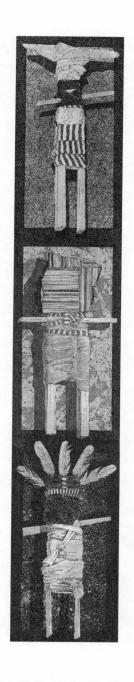

PROLOGUE

Stone Hammer Poem

1.

This stone
become a hammer
of stone, this maul

is the colour
of bone (no,
bone is the colour
of this stone maul).

The rawhide loops
are gone, the
hand is gone, the
buffalo's skull
is gone;

the stone is
shaped like the skull
of a child.

2.

This paperweight on my desk

where I begin
this poem   was

found in a wheatfield
lost (this hammer,
this poem).

Cut to a function,
this stone was
(the hand is   gone—

3.

Grey, two-headed,
the pemmican maul

fell from the travois or
a boy playing   lost it in
the prairie wool or
a woman   left it in
the brain of a buffalo or

it is a million
years older than
the hand that
chipped stone or
raised slough
water (or blood) or

4.

This stone maul
was found.

In the field
my grandfather
thought
was his

my father
thought was his

5.

It is a stone
old as the last
Ice Age, the
retreating/the
recreating ice,
the retreating
buffalo, the
retreating Indians

(the saskatoons bloom
white (infrequently
the chokecherries the
highbush cranberries the
pincherries bloom
white along the barbed
wire fence (the
pemmican   winter

6.

This stone maul
stopped a plough
long enough for one
Gott im Himmel.

The Blackfoot (the
Cree?) not

finding the maul
cursed.

? did he curse
? did he try to
go back
? what happened
I have to/I want
to know (not know)
? WHAT HAPPENED

7.

The poem
is the stone
chipped and hammered
until it is shaped
like the stone
hammer, the maul.

8.

Now the field is
mine because
I gave it
(for a price)

to a young man
(with a growing son)
who did not

notice that the land
did not belong

to the Indian who
gave it to the Queen
(for a price) who
gave it to the CPR
(for a price) which
gave it to my grandfather
(for a price) who
gave it to my father
(50 bucks an acre
Gott im Himmel I cut
down all the trees I
picked up all the stones) who

gave it to his son
(who sold it)

ROBERT KROETSCH

9.

This won't
surprise you.

My grandfather
lost the stone maul.

10.

My father (retired)
grew raspberries.
He dug in his potato patch.
He drank one glass of wine
each morning.
He was lonesome
for death.

He was lonesome for the
hot wind on his face, the smell
of horses, the distant
hum of a threshing machine,
the oilcan he carried, the weight
of a crescent wrench in his hind pocket.

He was lonesome for his absent
son and his daughters,
for his wife, for his own
brothers and sisters and
his own mother and father.

He found the stone maul
on a rockpile in the
north-west corner of what
he thought of
as his wheatfield.

He kept it (the
stone maul) on the railing
of the back porch in
a raspberry basket.

II.

I keep it
on my desk
(the stone).

Sometimes I use it
in the (hot) wind
(to hold down paper)

smelling a little of cut
grass or maybe even of
ripening wheat or of
buffalo blood hot
in the dying sun.

Sometimes I write
my poems for that

stone hammer.

I —————————————————— FIELD NOTES

the   the ledger survived
ledger
                       because it was neither
itself   human nor useful

a. "in bookkeeping, the book of final entry, in which a record of
    debits, credits, and all money transactions is kept."

                                    the
                                    book
                                    of
                                    columns

page 33: James Darling

1880

Mar 22: to sawing square timber   1.44
June 21: to 1 round cedar bed   3.50
June 21: to 1 jack shingles   .50
Dec 4: to sawing mable [*sic*]   1.50   Nov 4/82 by logs   4.10

                                            (it doesn't balance)

some pages torn out (
by accident)
some pages remaining (
by accident)

page 62: Nicholas Neubecker

1893

Nov 16: to chopping 8 bags   .40
Dec 19: to chopping 880 lbs   .49
        : to elm scantling   .18

                            the poet: by accident
                            finding in the torn ledger

                            (IT DOESN'T BALANCE)

the green poem:

my grandfather, Henry (dead)   the ledger itself (surviving)
in his watermill (gone)   purchased in the Bruce County
on the Teeswater River,   Drug and Book Store (Price:
on the road between Formosa $1.00 PAID, the leather cover
and Belmore,   brown. In gold:
needing a new ledger: THE LEDGER:

                                    EVERYTHING I WRITE
                                    I SAID, IS A SEARCH
                                    (is debit, is credit)

is a search   for some pages

                    remaining

            (by accident)

the poet: finding   the column straight
in the torn ledger   the column broken

            FINDING

everything you write
my wife, my daughters, said   *the book of final entry*
is a search   for the dead   *in which a record is kept.*

b.   "a horizontal piece of timber secured to the uprights
       supporting the putlogs in a scaffolding, or the like."

The Canada Gazette, August 17, 1854:
"Notice is hereby given that the undermentioned lands ... in the
County of Bruce, U.C., will be open for sale to actual settlers ...
The price to be Ten shillings per acre ... Actual occupation to be
Immediate and continuous ..."

                              To raise a barn;

cut down a forest.

                              To raise oats and hay;

burn the soil.

                              To raise cattle and hogs;

kill the bear   "As to the climate of the dis-
kill the mink   trict, Father Holzer cannot
kill the marten   praise it enough. He declares
kill the lynx   that during the first nine
kill the fisher   months of his residence here
kill the beaver   they had only one funeral, and
kill the moose   that was of a man 84 years old."

                              A Pristine Forest
                                    A Pristine Forest

"That winter, therefore, timbers of elm and maple and pine were
cut the necessary lengths, hewed and dressed and hauled by means
of the oxen to the barn site. Cedar logs were sawn in suitable
lengths and shingles split from these blocks ..."

was the cry that spread.

Henry, the elder of the two
brothers, was born in 1856,
across the river from the mill

Shaping the trees
into logs (burn
the slash) into
timbers and planks.

in a log shanty measuring (as
specified in *The Canada Ga-
zette*, August 17, 1854) at least
sixteen feet by eighteen.

Shaping the trees
into ledgers.
Raising the barn.

That they might sit down
a forest had fallen.

to a pitcher of Formosa beer

Shaping the trees.
Into shingles.
Into scantling.
Into tables and chairs.

Have a seat, John.
Sit down, Henry.

That they might sit down
a forest had fallen.

page 119: John O. Miller, brickmaker in Mildmay

1888

Aug 17: to cedar shingles   12.50   Aug 17: by Brick 2500
                                                    At 50¢   12.50

(I'll be damned. It balances.)

yes:no
no:yes

"... a specimen of the self-made men who have made Canada
what it is, and of which no section has brought forth more or better
representatives than the County of Bruce. Mr. Miller was never an
office-seeker, but devoted himself strictly and energetically to the
pursuit of his private business, and on his death was the owner of a
very large and valuable property ... "

Shaping the trees.
Pushing up daisies.

Have another glass, John.
Ja, ja. What the hell.

What's the matter, John?
My bones ache.

Take a day off, John.
No time.

A horizontal piece of timber
supporting the putlogs
in a scaffolding, or the like.

(specimens of the self-made
men who have made Canada
what it is)

The barn is still standing
(the mill, however, is gone)
sound as the day it was raised.

No time.
August 17, 1888.

No time.

Shaping the trees.
Pushing up daisies.

I'll be damned.
It balances.

c.   "one who is permanently or constantly in a place; a resident.
      Obs."

"Old Gottlieb Haag was a man
verging on 80 years of age. As
a young man he had emigrated
from Germany to America to
seek his fortune and better his

condition in the New World. Leaving Rotterdam in a sailing ship bound for New York, after a tedious and tempestuous voyage in which his ship was frequently blown half-way back to Europe, he finally landed on the shores of the New World. Here all his fortune lay before him."

(*Das ist doch nicht möglich!*)

arrivals: the sailing ship
arrivals: the axe
arrivals: the almighty dollar

departures: the trout stream
departures: the passenger-pigeon
departures: the pristine forest

arrivals: the stump fence
arrivals: the snake fence
arrivals: the stone fence

(Here all his fortune lay before him)

"As a sample of the condition of many of the early settlers on their arrival, the Clement family (who came from the Niagara frontier, crossing rivers on rafts and swimming their cattle) possessed only two axes, a hoe, ox-yoke, log-chain, a "drag" made from the crotch of a tree, and an "ox-jumper" in the way of agricultural implements; and, as things went in those days, this was considered a first-rate stock. Though very few families in this country ever suffered any inconvenience or annoyances from the aborigines, the Clements were rather roughly used by a wandering band on one occasion, who forcibly took possession of the whole roof of their shanty (which was composed chiefly of birch-bark) for the purpose of canoe-making."

departures: the birch-bark
canoe
(ledger: a resident.
Obsolete.)

Census, 1861: County of Bruce:

2,663 horses   turnips: 848,403 bushels
6,274 working oxen   wheat: 642,110 bushels
19,830 cattle of all ages   maple sugar: 170,365 lbs
29,412 sheep and swine   cheese: 24,324 lbs

The enumerator "got his feet frozen
and another had to finish the work.
Both made oath to their respective
sheets and these are numbered and
designated separately."

Census, 1861: Township of Carrick:

"Indians if any"   Name: Catherine Schneider
                          Year of birth: 1841
                          Place of birth: Atlantic Ocean

                          Place of birth: Atlantis,
                          the kingdom sought
                          beyond the stone gates,
          none   beyond the old home,
                          beyond the ceaseless
                          wars of the Rhine
                          Palatinate. The sought
                          continent of fortune
                          lying beyond
Gottlieb Haag's only son your father's recurring
grew up to be the first man nightmare of the (forced)
hanged for murder   march to Moscow
in the County of Bruce   (my bones ache),
                          beyond the flight
(I can't believe my eyes.) from the burning
                          fields. Beyond

having, on a wintry night, in
a sleigh box on the road from
Belmore to Formosa, clubbed
to death his rival

the night of terror
crossing the closed
border. *Atlantis*:
the kingdom dreamed

(I can't believe my eyes.)

in love.

DEPARTURES:

DEPARTURES:

"It is well watered by the south
branch of the Saugeen and a
number of tributaries, which af-
ford fine mill privileges almost in
every section."

Henry, on quiet days at the
mill, on wintry days, made fur-
niture for sale to the thriving
inhabitants who intended to
stay.

page 95: Mr. Peter Brick

1880

1881

Dec. 5: to 1 bed	4.00		
" " 6 chairs	4.50		
" " 2 "	1.00		
" " 1 sink	4.00		
" " 1 dressing case	16.00		
" " 1 sideboard	10.00		
" " 1 table	4.00	Settelt [*sic*]	
	43.50	by 1 horse	43.50

Mr. Peter Brick, on the road
from Belmore to Formosa,
intending to stay ("Beer
also was plentiful and cheap.")

bought new furniture for his
new brick house and turned

the old log shanty into
a summer kitchen where
on hot afternoons
he might   wait out the heat.

ledger: a resident.
Pushing up daisies.
Obsolete.

d. "the nether millstone."

They were draining the pond to do
some work on the dam. Seeing a few
fish at the floodgate, Henry sent one of
his sons for a bucket. The boy, step-
ping into the water, catching fish with
his bare hands, filled the bucket.
Henry could hardly believe his eyes.
But he sent the boy for a sack. And
couldn't believe. But sent the boy for a
tub, for a barrel.

Joe Hauck got his arm caught in the water-wheel.
He screamed. But no one heard him.

He couldn't get free. The wheel was trying to
lift him up to heaven. He couldn't get free.

Joe Hauck had a good head on his shoulders, a
cap on his head. He threw his cap into the racing

water. The men unloading logs below the mill
noticed the cap; they ran on up to the millsite.

The doctor had good horses; he got there that same
day. Three men held Joe Hauck flat on a table,

right next to a saw, while the doctor patched
and sewed, ran out of thread, broke a needle.

to
chopping
8
bags

.40

you must see
the confusion again
the chaos   again
the original forest

under the turning wheel
the ripened wheat, the
razed forest, the wrung
man: the nether stone

page 117: Paul Willie

1893

by 1/2 Day Work	.38
" work with team	2.00
" 100 lbs of flour	1.85
" 25 bushels lime	3.12
" plowing potato patch	1.50
" working at dam	2.00
Team to Mildmay	.50
by 5 cord of wood	8.00
" beef 87 lbs at 5¢	4.35
" hay 1,000 lbs	4.00
" 2 hemlock logs	.75
" 1 20-ft cedar log	.50
" 3 16-ft cedar	.75

it doesn't balance

1854 to 1910:

to sawing	Butternut
" "	Pine
" "	Basswood
" "	Birch
" "	Soft Elm
" "	Rock Elm
" "	Cedar
" "	Tamarack
" "	Maple
" "	Beech
" "	Black Ash
" "	Hemlock
" "	Cherry

it doesn't balance

The bottom of the pond was not so much mud as fish. The receding water was a wide fountain of leaping fish; Henry sent a daughter to go fetch Charlie Reinhart, Ignatz Kiefer, James Darling, Peter Brick. The neighbours began to arrive (and strangers, bearing empty sacks) from up the road to Formosa, from down the road to Belmore; the neighbours came with tubs and barrels, with a wagon box, and they clubbed at the eels that skated on the bright mud. They lunged at the leaping trout. They pounced like bullfrogs after bullfrogs. And they swam in the quick, receding flood.

the grinding stone
that does not
turn:

under the turning
stone: the nether
stone: the ledger

intending to stay

Completed Field Notes

The children screamed after their leaping, swimming parents. They didn't believe their eyes. They bathed in the clean, the original mud. They flung the fish onto dry land and themselves stayed in the water: they usurped the fish. The floodgate was open, the dam no longer a dam. They rose, blue-eyed and shouting, out of the tripping, slippery mud: while the fish, their quick gills strange to the sudden air, drowned for lack of water.

The children, sitting hunched on the dam,
hearing Joe Hauck scream, were silent.

In all their lives they had never heard Joe Hauck
scream (his arm mangled: by the turning wheel).

People said Joe Hauck was never the same
after that water-wheel tried lifting him

up to heaven. No matter what he did, people shook
their heads. "He's not the same," they said.

When his brothers went west to homestead, Joe
elected to stay at the mill. He wasn't the same.

e.   "a large flat stone, esp. one laid over a tomb."

> *Dear Bob,*
>
> *... In regards to information about my Grandmother—your*
> *great Grandmother—Theresia Tschirhart. She was a sedate tall*
> *heavy-set person, well read and could visit with the best. She did*
> *love reading and mixing with people. She was widowed three*
> *times before going west ... She passed away after trying to sit on*
> *a chair and missing it, broke her hip and was in bed for a few*
> *weeks, died and was buried in Spring Lake, Alberta. She was*
> *still very active before her fall ...*
>
> > *all my love*
> > *Aunt Mary O'C*

born in Alsace, she spoke
German with a French accent,
English with a German accent,

looked down on all Bavarians
for being the tree-chopping
beer drinkers they all were:

Married three Bavarians.
Buried three Bavarians.   it balances

What did most men feel
in her presence?   Terror.

What did they do about it?   Proposed.

                                           (I can't
                                           believe my eyes)

An A-1 cook.
Kept a spotless house.
She wasn't just careful,
she was tight.
Went to church more often   Men felt terror.
than was necessary.   They proposed.

                                           Census, 1861
                                           County of Bruce:
                                           Deaths in 1860
                                           (Age and Cause):

                                           1 yr: croup
                                           blank: born dead
                                           5 months: fits
                                           blank: dysentery
                                           16 yrs: hurt
                                           by sawmill wheel
                                           38: 1 Deth
                                           Inflammation

                                           Henry's father: dead
                                           (The doctor had good
                                           horses)

page 88: John Mosack

in a/c Theresia ~~Kroetsch Messner~~ Hauck

Jan 19: to white ash   12.05   PAID IN FULL
Aug 24: to black ash   2.84   PAID IN FULL
Nov 10: to pine 216 ft   2.16   PAID IN FULL

Owing that woman money
was a mistake.

What do I owe you?
Seventeen dollars and five cents.
What'll you settle for?   You MUST
Seventeen dollars and five cents.   marry the terror.

Finally succumbed to the grave herself.
Spring Lake, Alberta. 1913. *Ruhe in
Frieden*.

The Canadian climate:
a short summer
followed by a short winter
followed by a short summer
followed by a short winter

ROBERT KROETSCH

24

She was a ring-tailed snorter   (you must marry
just the same.   the terror)

1913
1829
———
  84

Cause of death: She lies buried to the east
                                   of the church in Spring Lake,
went to sit down   Alberta. She was visiting in
and missed the chair   Heisler, Alberta, at the time
                                   of her death: Heisler was so
                                   new it didn't have a graveyard:

                                   DEATH PROHIBITED
Verdammt!   ON THESE PREMISES

What do I owe you?

O bury me not
on the lone prairie.

WHAT DO I OWE YOU?
WHAT DO I OWE YOU?

Where the coyotes howl
and the wind blows free.

Even by-God dead
washed
dressed
laid out   her desire to be interred
she indicated   in the plot of Ontario earth
(she was a ring-tailed   next to the ledger that
snorter just the same)   covered her first husband:

zum andenken von

LORENZ KROETSCH

gestorben den
13th Feb 1860
alt 38 Jahre

Ruhe nun im sanften schlummer   inflammation
In der erde kühlem schoos   of
Hier entwichen allem kummer   the
Ist der friede nun dein loos   lungs:
Noch umringen wir dein grab   coughed
Schauen wehmuts voll hinab   gagged
Doch zur ruhe gehn auch wir   choked
Gott sie dank wir folgen dir.   died.

Requiescat in Pace

No one would pay the shot.
The CPR wouldn't do it   An Alberta grave
for love.   is a cold, cold grave.

f. "a book that lies permanently in some place."

A man that lies permanently in some place.
A woman that lies permanently in some place.
A resident. *Obsolete.*
The book of final entry.

The book
of columns.
The book that lies
permanently.

The timber supporting the putlogs
in a scaffolding:

e.g., the poem   in the chaos

in the dark night
in the beautiful forest

"With no effort or pretension to literary merit, the object will be rather to present a plain statement of facts of general interest which bear upon the past growth and development of this wonderfully prosperous section of the Province, in such manner as to render future comparisons more easy, and offer to the rising generation an incentive to emulation in the examples of the pioneers, whose self-reliant industry and progressive enterprise have conquered the primeval forests, and left in their stead, as a heritage to posterity, a country teeming with substantial comforts and material wealth, and reflecting in its every feature the indomitable spirit and true manliness of a noble race, whose lives and deeds will shine while the communities they have founded shall continue to exist."

Gottlieb Haag's only son   (with no effort
(for the first murder
in the County of Bruce)   or pretension
Hanged.   to literary merit)

"Caoutchouc usually mowed down three or four spellers. When it didn't, such words as gubernatorial or phthisicky or threnody would do the trick."

Henry. How do you spell maple?   m-a-b-l-e

Henry. How do you spell balance?   b-a-l-l-o-n-s

Henry. How do you spell Henry?   H-e-n-e-r-y

    Threnody:
    a song
    of lamentation.

    the ledger itself
    survives

page 69: Edward McGue   intending to stay

1886

to hemlock rafters   5.01
to cedar shakes   18.75   the roof over his head

1887

to hemlock fencing   5.10
to 1 plow   9.15   the sod beneath his boots

    the ledger stone
    the nether stone

    either would do
    the lasting trick

    the stone singing
    song on the stone

Robert Nickel
John Molloy
Jacob Sagmiller
PAID IN FULL
Luke Steigler
Pat Mahoney
George Straus
PAID IN FULL
Fleming Ballogh
Michel Kirby
Robert Curl
PAID IN FULL
John Elder
Michael Laporte
Richard McDaniel
PAID IN FULL
Christian Kirschmer
Henry Busby
William Trench
PAID IN FULL
Joseph Hall
Peter Shoemaker
David Rush
PAID IN FULL

the ledger itself

      surviving

beyond the last felling
beyond the last tree felled
the last turn of the wheel
the last coin worn and gone
from the last pocket
worn

and gone
beyond the last turned page
beyond the last

    entry

ROBERT KROETSCH

"They had to cut down three trees in order
to bury the first man dead in Formosa."

Some people go to heaven.
Some people write poems.
Some people go west
to homestead.

Cut to the rock
the rock rose up.
Tombstones are hard
to kill.

REST IN PEACE
You Must Marry the Terror

Seed Catalogue

I.

No. 176 — *Copenhagen Market Cabbage*: "This *new introduction,
strictly speaking,* is in every respect a *thoroughbred,* a *cabbage* of *highest
pedigree,* and is *creating considerable flurry* among *professional gardeners*
all *over the world."*

We took the storm windows/off
the south side of the house
and put them on the hotbed.
Then it was spring. Or, no:
then winter was ending.

> "I wish to say we had lovely success
> this summer with the seed purchased
> of you. We had the finest Sweet
> Corn in the county, and Cabbage
> were dandy."
> —W.W. Lyon, South Junction, Man.

> > My mother said:
> > Did you wash your ears?
> > You could grow cabbages
> > in those ears.

Winter was ending.
This is what happened:
we were harrowing the garden.
You've got to understand this:
I was sitting on the horse.
The horse was standing still.
I fell off.

> > The hired man laughed: how
> > in hell did you manage to
> > fall off a horse that was
> > *standing still?*

Bring me the radish seeds,
my mother whispered.

Into the dark of January
the seed catalogue bloomed

a winter proposition, if
spring should come, then,

with illustrations:

No. 25 — *McKenzie's Improved Golden Wax Bean*: "THE MOST
PRIZED OF ALL BEANS. *Virtue* is its own reward. We have had
many expressions from *keen discriminating gardeners extolling our seed*
and *this variety*."

> Beans, beans,
> the musical fruit;
> the more you eat,
> the more you virtue.

My mother was marking the first row
with a piece of binder twine, stretched
between two pegs.

The hired man laughed: just
about planted the little bugger.
Cover him up and see what grows.

My father didn't laugh. He was puzzled
by any garden that was smaller than a
quarter-section of wheat and summerfallow.

the home place: N.E. 17-42-16-W4th Meridian.

the home place: one and a half miles west of Heisler, Alberta,
                on the correction line road
                and three miles south.

No trees
around the house.
Only the wind.
Only the January snow.
Only the summer sun.
The home place:
a terrible symmetry.

How do you grow a gardener?

> Telephone Peas
> Garden Gem Carrots
> Early Snowcap Cauliflower
> Perfection Globe Onions
> Hubbard Squash
> Early Ohio Potatoes

This is what happened—at my mother's wake. This
is a fact—the World Series was in progress. The
Cincinnati Reds were playing the Detroit Tigers.
It was raining. The road to the graveyard was barely
passable. The horse was standing still. Bring me
the radish seeds, my mother whispered.

2.

My father was mad at the badger: the badger was digging holes in
the potato patch, threatening man and beast with broken limbs (I
quote). My father took the double-barrelled shotgun out into the
potato patch and waited.

Every time the badger stood up, it looked like a little man, come out
of the ground. Why, my father asked himself—Why would so fine a
fellow live under the ground? Just for the cool of roots? The solace
of dark tunnels? The blood of gophers?

My father couldn't shoot the badger. He uncocked the shotgun,
came back to the house in time for breakfast. The badger dug an-
other hole. My father got mad again. They carried on like that all
summer.

Love is an amplification
by doing/over and over.

Love is a standing up
to the loaded gun.

Love is a burrowing.

One morning my father actually shot at the badger. He killed a magpie that was pecking away at a horse turd about fifty feet beyond and to the right of the spot where the badger had been standing.

A week later my father told the story again. In that version he intended to hit the magpie. Magpies, he explained, are a nuisance. They eat robins' eggs. They're harder to kill than snakes, jumping around the way they do, nothing but feathers.

Just call me sure-shot,
my father added.

3.

No. 1248 — *Hubbard Squash*: "As *mankind* seems to have a *particular fondness* for squash, *Nature* appears to have *especially* provided this *matchless* variety of *superlative flavour*."

Love is a leaping up
and down.

Love
is a beak in the warm flesh.

"As a cooker, it heads the list for warted squash. The vines are of strong running growth; the fruits are large, olive shaped, of a deep rich green colour, the rind is smooth ... "

But how do you grow a lover?

This is the God's own truth:
playing dirty is a mortal sin
the priest told us, you'll go to hell
and burn forever (with illustrations)—

it was our second day of catechism
—Germaine and I went home that
afternoon   if it's that bad, we
said to each other   we realized
we better quit   we realized

let's do it just one last time
and quit.

This is the God's own truth:
catechism, they called it,
the boys had to sit in the pews
on the right, the girls on the left.
Souls were like underwear that you

wore inside. If boys and girls sat
together—

Adam and Eve got caught
playing dirty.

This is the truth.
We climbed up into a granary
full of wheat   to the gunny sacks
the binder twine was shipped in—

we spread the paper from the sacks
smooth sheets   on the soft wheat
Germaine and I   we were like/one

we had discovered, don't ask me
how, where—but when the priest said
playing dirty we knew—well—

he had named it   he had named
our world   out of existence
(the horse   was standing still)

—This is my first confession. Bless me father I played
    dirty so long, just the other day, up in the granary
    there by the car shed—up there on the Brantford Binder
    Twine gunny sacks and the sheets of paper—Germaine
    with her dress up and her bloomers down—

—Son. For penance, keep your peter in your pants
    for the next thirteen years.

But how—

        Adam and Eve and Pinch-Me
        went down to the river to swim—
        Adam and Eve got drownded.

But how do you grow a lover?

        We decided we could do it
        just one last time.

4.

It arrived in winter, the seed catalogue, on a January
day. It came into town on the afternoon train.

Mary Hauck, when she came west from Bruce County, Ontario,
arrived in town on a January day. She brought along
her hope chest.

She was cooking in the Heisler Hotel. The Heisler Hotel
burned down on the night of June 21, 1919. Everything
in between: lost. Everything: an absence

of satin sheets
of embroidered pillowcases
of tea-towels and English china
of silver serving spoons.

How do you grow a prairie town?

> The gopher was the model.
> Stand up straight:
> telephone poles
> grain elevators
> church steeples.
> Vanish, suddenly: the
> gopher was the model.

How do you grow a past/
to live in

the absence of silkworms
the absence of clay and wattles (whatever the hell
    they are)
the absence of Lord Nelson
the absence of kings and queens
the absence of a bottle opener, and me with a vicious
    attack of the 26-ounce flu
the absence of both Sartre and Heidegger
the absence of pyramids
the absence of lions
the absence of lutes, violas and xylophones
the absence of a condom dispenser in the Lethbridge Hotel and
    me about to screw an old Blood whore. I was
    in love.
the absence of the Parthenon, not to mention the Cathédrale de
    Chartres
the absence of psychiatrists
the absence of sailing ships
the absence of books, journals, daily newspapers and everything
    else but the *Free Press Prairie Farmer* and *The
    Western Producer*
the absence of gallows (with apologies to Louis Riel)
the absence of goldsmiths
the absence of the girl who said that if the Edmonton Eskimos
    won the Grey Cup she'd let me kiss her
    nipples in the foyer of the Palliser Hotel. I
    don't know where she got to.
the absence of Heraclitus

the absence of the Seine, the Rhine, the Danube, the Tiber and
the Thames. Shit, the Battle River ran dry
one fall. The Strauss boy could piss across it.
He could piss higher on a barn wall than any
of us. He could piss right clean over the
principal's new car.
the absence of ballet and opera
the absence of Aeneas

How do you grow a prairie town?

Rebuild the hotel when it burns down. Bigger. Fill it
full of a lot of A-1 Hard Northern Bullshitters.

— You ever hear the one about the woman who buried
her husband with his ass sticking out of the ground
so that every time she happened to walk by she could
give it a swift kick?

— Yeh, I heard it.

5.

I planted some melons, just to see what would
happen. Gophers ate everything.

I applied to the Government.
I wanted to become a postman,
to deliver real words
to real people.

There was no one to receive
my application

I don't give a damn if I do die do die do die do die do die
do die do die do die do die do die do die do die do die do
die do die do die do die do die do die do die do die do die
do

6.

No. 339 — *McKenzie's Pedigreed Early Snowcap Cauliflower*: "Of the many *varieties* of *vegetables* in *existence*, *Cauliflower* is *unquestionably* one of the *greatest inheritances* of the *present generation, particularly Western Canadians*. There is *no place* in the *world* where *better cauliflowers* can be *grown* than right here in the *West*. The *finest specimens* we have *ever seen*, larger and of *better quality*, are *annually grown* here on our *prairies*. Being *particularly* a *high altitude plant* it *thrives* to a *point* of *perfection* here, *seldom seen* in *warmer climes*."

But how do you grow a poet?

Start: with an invocation
invoke—

His muse is
his muse/if
memory is

and you have
no memory then
no meditation
no song (shit
we're up against it)

          how about that girl
          you felt up in the
          school barn or that
          girl you necked with
          out by Hastings' slough
          and ran out of gas with
          and nearly froze to
          death with/or that
          girl in the skating
          rink shack who had on
          so much underwear you
          didn't have enough
          prick to get past her/
          CCM skates

Once upon a time in the village of Heisler—

—Hey, wait a minute.
That's a story.

How do you grow a poet?

> For appetite: cod-liver
> oil.
> For bronchitis: mustard
> plasters.
> For pallor and failure to fill
> the woodbox: sulphur
> & molasses.
> For self-abuse: ten Our
> Fathers & ten Hail Marys.
> For regular bowels: Sunny Boy
> Cereal.

How do you grow a poet?

"It's a pleasure to advise that I
won the First Prize at the Calgary
Horticultural Show ... This is my
first attempt. I used your seeds."

> Son, this is a crowbar.
> This is a willow fencepost.
> This is a sledge.
> This is a roll of barbed wire.
> This is a bag of staples.
> This is a claw hammer.

We give form to this land by running
a series of posts and three strands
of barbed wire around a quarter-section.

> First off I want you to take that
> crowbar and driver 1,156 holes
> in that gumbo.
> And the next time you want to
> write a poem
> we'll start the haying.

How do you grow a poet?

> This is a prairie road.
> This road is the shortest distance
> Between nowhere and nowhere.
> This road is a poem.
>
> Just two miles up the road
> you'll find a porcupine
> dead in the ditch. It was
> trying to cross the road.

As for the poet himself
we can find no record
of his having traversed
the land/in either direction

no trace of his coming
or going/only a scarred
page, a spoor of wording
a reduction to mere black

and white/a pile of rabbit
turds that tells us
all spring long
where the track was

poet ... say uncle.

How?

Rudy Wiebe: "You must lay great black steel lines of
fiction, break up that space with huge design and, like
the fiction of the Russian steppes, build a giant
artifact. No song can do that ..."

February 14, 1976. Rudy, you
took us there: to the Oldman River
Lorna & Byrna, Ralph & Steve and me
you showed us where
the Bloods surprised the Crees
in the next coulee/surprised
them to death. And after
you showed us Rilke's word
Lebensgliedes.

Rudy: Nature thou art.

7.

Brome Grass (Bromus Inermis): "No amount of cold will kill it. It
withstands the summer suns. Water may stand on it for several
weeks without apparent injury. The roots push through the soil,
throwing up new plants continually. It *starts quicker* than other
grasses in the spring. *Remains green* longer in the fall. *Flourishes un-
der absolute neglect.*"

The end of winter:
seeding/time.

*How do you grow
a poet?*

(a)

I was drinking with Al Purdy. We went round and round
in the restaurant on top of the Chateau Lacombe. We
were the turning centre in the still world, the winter
of Edmonton was hardly enough to cool our out-sights.

The waitress asked us to leave. She was rather insistent;
we were bad for business, shouting poems at the paying
customers. Twice, Purdy galloped a Cariboo horse
right straight through the dining area.

Now that's what I call
a piss-up.

"No song can do that."

(b)

No. 2362—*Imperialis Morning
Glory*: "This is the wonderful *Jap-
anese Morning Glory*, celebrated the
world over for its *wondrous beauty*
of both flowers and foliage."

Sunday, January 12, 1975. This evening after
rereading *The Double Hook*: looking at Japanese prints.
Not at actors. Not at courtesans. Rather: Hiroshige's
series, *Fifty-Three Stations on the Tokaido*.

From the *Tokaido* series: "Shono-Haku-u." The
bare-assed travellers, caught in a sudden shower.
Men and trees, bending. How it is in a rain shower/
that you didn't see coming. And couldn't have avoided/
even if you had.

> The double hook:
> The home place.

> The stations of the way:
> The other garden

> *Flourishes.*
> *Under absolute neglect.*

(c)

Jim Bacque said (I was waiting for a plane,
after a reading; Terminal 2, Toronto)—he said,
You've got to deliver the pain to some woman,
don't you?

—Hey, Lady.
   You at the end of the bar.
   I wanna tell you something.

—Yuh?

—Pete Knight—of Crossfield,
   Alberta. Bronc-Busting Champion
   of the World. You ever hear of
   Pete Knight, the King of All
   Cowboys, Bronc-Busting Champion
   of the world?

—Huh-uh.

—You know what I mean? King
   of *All* Cowboys ... Got
   killed—by a horse.
   He fell off.

—You some kind of nut
   or something?

8.

            We silence words
            by writing them down.

THIS IS THE LAST WILL AND TESTAMENT
OF ME, HENRY L. KROETSCH:

(a) [yes, his first bequest]

To my son Frederick my carpenter tools.

It was his first bequest. First,
a man must build.

Those horse-barns around Heisler—
those perfectly designed barns
with the rounded roofs—only Freddie
knew how to build them. He mapped
the parklands with perfect horse-barns.

> I remember my Uncle Freddie.
> (The farmers no longer
> use horses.)
>
> Back in the 30s, I remember
> he didn't have enough money
> to buy a pound of coffee.
>
> Every morning at breakfast
> he drank a cup of hot water
> with cream and sugar in it.
>
> Why, I asked him one morning—
> I wasn't all that old—why
> do you do that? I asked him.
>
> Jesus Christ, he said. He was
> a gentle man, really. Don't you
> understand *anything*?

9.

The danger of merely living.

a shell/exploding
in the black sky: a
strange planting

a bomb/exploding
in the earth: a
strange

man/falling
on the city.
Killed him dead.

It was a strange
planting.

the absence of my cousin who was shot down while bombing
the city that was his maternal great-grandmother's
birthplace. He was the navigator. He guided himself
to that fatal occasion:

> — a city he had
>   forgotten
> — a woman he had
>   forgotten

He intended merely to release a cargo of bombs on a
target and depart. The exploding shell was:

a) an intrusion on a design that was not his, or

b) an occurrence which he had in fact, unintentionally,
    himself designed, or

c) it is essential that we understand this matter
    because:

He was the first descendant of that family to return
to the Old Country. He took with him: a cargo of bombs.

> Anna Weller: *Geboren* Köln, 1849.
> Kenneth MacDonald: Died Cologne, 1943.

> A terrible symmetry.

A strange muse: forgetfulness. Feeding her far children
to ancestral guns, blasting them out of the sky, smack/
into the earth. Oh, she was the mothering sort. Blood/
on her green thumb.

10.

After the bomb/blossoms
After the city/falls
After the rider/falls
(the horse
standing still)

Poet, teach us
to love our dying.

West is a winter place.
The palimpsest of prairie

under the quick erasure
of snow, invites a flight.

How/do you grow a garden?

(a)

> No. 3060 — *Spencer Sweet Pea*:
> Pkt $.10; oz $.25;
> quarter lb $.75; half lb $1.25.

Your sweet peas
climbing the staked
chicken wire,
climbing the stretched
binder twine by
the front porch

taught me the smell
of morning, the grace
of your tired
hands, the strength
of a noon sun, the
colour of prairie grass

taught me the smell
of my sweating armpits.

(b)

How do you a garden grow?
How do you grow a garden?

"Dear Sir,

The longest brome grass I remember seeing was one night in Brooks. We were on our way up to the Calgary Stampede, and reached Brooks about 11 P.M., perhaps earlier because there was still a movie on the drive-in screen. We unloaded Cindy, and I remember tying her up to the truck box and the brome grass was up to her hips. We laid down in the back of the truck—on some grass I pulled by hand—and slept for about three hours, then drove into Calgary.

Amie"

(c)

No trees
around the house,
only the wind.
Only the January snow.
Only the summer sun.

Adam and Eve got drownded—
Who was left?

How I Joined the Seal Herd

I swear it was not   the hearing
itself   I first refused
it was   the sight of my ears

in the mirror: the sight
of my ears   was the first
clue: my head did not please me

the seals so loud   I could hardly
accept the message: she wanted
no other going/than to be gone   the

neat bed itself   strange in the
mirror, she   kneeling across the bed
to close the window: maybe

I have this wrong: but only then
I saw   my ears/the difference
she wanted to go   I heard

a loud snort   a throaty grunt:
it was the breeding season   the tide
low, the wind still: they'd be wary

I knew, the seals   lying together
in the hot sun   maybe 300 seals
I counted   slipping off my shoes

the effect was immediate   I learned
to let my body give   it was not I
who controlled the rocks   I learned

curling my stockinged toes   to the
granite cracks and edges: maybe
I have this wrong   but I knew

in the first instant   of my courage
I must undo my very standing/crawl
on the wet rocks, the sand   not

standing   ease down on my belly:
it was strange at first   looking up
at the world: but I arched my back

I turned my head and paused   what
was I doing there on the beach/   wait
the luminous eyes of a young   seal cow:

I, the lone bull seal   bravely
guarding the rookery   alone
holding together a going world/   but

frankly, I wanted to get laid   she was
maybe five feet tall (long)   the cow:
I could see   she didn't like my clothes/

moving carefully   avoiding any fuss
I unbuttoned, I unzipped   squirmed
out of my shorts, my socks   it was, yes

quite frankly   love at first sight/
flicking, with my left hand   some sand
over my back   for an instant

I thought of my wallet   my driver's
licence, my credit cards: she had dark
fur on her belly   a delicate nose:

she went towards the water   looking
back over her shoulder/   the water
looking iceberg cold   I wasn't quite ready

she was rushing me: men in their forties
I shouted after her   are awfully good
in bed (on a sandbank   I corrected myself)

alone   I lay in the sand, I lay
watching   the slow coming of each wave
to the merciful shore   I humped

down to the water's curl   I, yes
without thinking,   *without thinking*, I
dove   my ears shrank

back   to my badly designed skull: under
the water: opening my eyes   I saw
the school of herring   SNAP

I had one in my teeth   I surfaced
hungry   I let myself float head up
on the lifting waves   I hauled out

I lolled: the cow that nudged me
awake: she might have been just plain
curious: my ear-flaps, my exterior testicles/

that crossed my mind   or slightly perverse
but the sun had warmed me again   we were both
well   I was still a man, I had to talk:

my nights are all bloody   I whispered
god, I am lonely   as a lover/my
naked body swims   in the leak of light

death has a breath too   it smells
of bedclothes   it smells of locked
windows   my nights are all drenched/

my body/I   saw she had no idea
well/that was nicer, even   than the
moist hunger   in her eyes

I brushed   at my grey beard/
my flipper   trying to make the hairs
look like   vibrissae (I believe is the word)

I wasn't quite ready when   the bull hit me
I whirled   caught at his neck
in my teeth   roared at the sonofabitch

slammed my head   against his nose:
he was gone/   the cow had noticed
everything   I could tell/she would

dance now/first   dance, slapping
the rising tide   to a quick froth:
she/I   rolling the waves themselves

back to the sea   I dared beyond the
last limit   of whatever I thought
I was   where, exactly, I asked, is—

my only question   and when she gave
herself/took   me out of the seen land
this, for the gone world   I sang:

America was a good lay   she nearly
fucked me to death, wow   but this
I'm a new man   (mammal, I corrected

myself) here   and yet I was going
too far   too far past everything
dispersed past   everything here/gone

dear, I whispered   (words again,
words)   I wanted to say/I am
writing   this poem   with my life

I whispered,   I hope (the rising
tide had lifted my socks   had swum
them to where   I might reach)

dear, I whispered   I hope my children
(ours, I corrected myself)   their ears perfect
will look   exactly like both of us.

(a)

and	even if it's true, that my women all have new lovers, then laugh, go ahead
but	don't expect me to cry
and	believe you me I have a few tricks up my sleeve myself
but	I'm honest, I'm nothing if not honest; a friend of mine in Moose Jaw who shall remain anonymous tells me he met the girl from Swift Current who scorned my offer of sex in a tree house; a bird in the hand, he said, joking, of course
and	flapped his arms
but	she didn't speak, she told him nothing, at least not a particular of her need for me
and	I didn't let on that I got the message
but	I recognized in an instant that I'd been the cause of her sweating, her shortness of breath
and	true, I'd be off like a shot to see her
but	the woman in Montreal is not so evasive, not so given to outright lies, deceptions
and	when she gets the letter I wrote last night, she'll say
but	darling, I was following a fire truck
and	quite by accident found the divine, ha, flicker
but	if I don't even bother to mail the letter she'll learn what it feels like to be ignored
and	the girl from Swift Current, the woman, can go climb a tree, I'm human too, you know, no slur intended

51

(b)

but	frankly
and	I don't think a little frankness would kill any of us, I had my peek into the abyss, my brush with the verities, such as they are, my astounding fall from innocence, you better believe it

but	I'm all right, don't feel you should worry, the responsibility is mine, I can take care of myself
and	the next time you feel like deceiving someone, why not try yourself
but	I have my work to sustain me, my poetry, the satisfaction of a job well done
and	even if I don't get the recognition I deserve, so what, who cares
but	time will tell: I keep thinking of Melville, who nearly went mad, possibly did, out of sheer neglect
and	Van Gogh; I guess you've heard that one, ha
but	the woman from Swift Current who didn't have the decency to say goodbye, she'll get her just reward; there's a reckoning in this world, you bet you me

(c)

and	virtue will out; I have my integrity; I know my own worth
but	I do have feelings, just because I'm a poet doesn't mean I have no feelings of my own, poets are human; I am, you might say, a kind of Phoenician, with reference, that is, to my trading in language, even in, to stretch a point, ha, my being at sea
and	the Phoenicians gave us the whole works
but	what does that matter to a world that ignores them, the Greeks got all the credit of course, because they stole the alphabet
and	the girl from Swift Current, she more or less took everything
but	the kitchen sink, claiming all my books, my records, my prints; she moved in with that photographer from Saskatoon, the one who takes those sterling pictures of the wind
and	I should sue
but	she follows large flocks of birds, I hear, calling my name
and	pleading

(d)

but   why she developed a thing for adverbs, that's too rich
            for my blood, I want to tell you
and   shortly she'll repent, *ha*
but   I do respect her privacy
and   as for the one who runs after doorknobs now: the world
            is not so round as she would have it, nor the door always
            hung to swing open
but   I keep my trap shut, I was dealt a tough mitt
and   any port in a storm they say: the dreamer, himself:
            lurching, leaping, flying; o to be mere gerund; no past,
            no future: what do you do in life: I ing
but   the door, cracked, opened; the lover who would, did; the
            night knelt into morning
and   is it not true that black is the absence of deceit
but   do not ask
and   asking, do not wait for the sun to bring light nor for
            the rain to fall, nor for women to remember, nor for
            interest to gather capital, nor for dictators to open
            gates, nor for laughter to win elections, nor for grey
            hair to darken, except in the earth
but   that's okay, we study
and   what we do not learn is how everything is: the exact
            colour of midnight varies, actually; the gin is not always,
            quite, insufficient; once a year a rubber breaks and we
            learn to count; the sun, in Tuktoyaktuk, disappears
            entirely for what should have been days
but   I'm all right now, don't feel you should worry

(e)

and   that brings to mind, if I might say so, my own sterling
            insights into the pseudonymous works of poor dear
            Kierkegaard, nagging his way into heaven, wiping his ass
            on the end of the world; he was no slouch with women,
            god knows
but   love hurt him; don't I know how he felt; just ask me

and	why not tell the truth: I, The Sad Phoenician of Love, slighted by the woman from—Nanaimo, I think it was, yes, Nanaimo—she who lives in a submarine
but	I gave her tat for tit
and	that reminds me, I owe myself a letter too, a gentle apology for sins of omission, ha, emission, well, let the chips fall
but	I was only joking when I suggested, we could go down together, hoo
and	a rose by any other name
but	let us call her A; she shall henceforth be referred to as A; right, eh
and	henceforth, everlastingly, A she shall be

(f)

but	I can see where some people might prefer just plain outright lies, as did Ms. R, the woman in Montreal, she who follows fires to firemen, who fell in love with a four-stroke engine
and	frankly, I'd be the last person on earth to criticize an interest in the mechanical world
but	there is nature, you know, there is such a thing as nature
and	I don't think anyone has ever been the worse for—well, I was going to say, a call of nature—I mean, a visit to nature
but	there is also artifice, of course, not to be confused with deception; i.e., on the one hand, a) the foot; on the other hand, b) the shoe
and	the shoes I'm wearing this morning, it just so happens, are a shade tight across the arch; not too tight, mind you
but	tight enough to be called tight; that is, the shoe on my right foot is a shade too tight, the shoe on my left foot fits like a glove
and	naturally I think of the foot as we refer to foot in the line of poetry; in the traditional line, that is
but	the poem must resist the poet, always, I can't help thinking

and	the woman in Nanaimo, she who lives in a submarine: the salmon creak at her window, the water her sky; x marks the known, the spot where she was
but	isn't

(g)

and	I'm sick of being galley slave to a penny's worth of words, sick of it; yes, I'm perfectly fine, except for a slight touch of mental prostration, dyspepsia, dropsy, consumption, bronchitis, the bleeding piles
but	they only hurt when I laugh, ha; despondency, spitting of blood, catarrh, a rare combination of dysentery
and	constipation, locomotor ataxy, hiccups, spermatorrhea, a hacking cough
but	I don't smoke, I'm too nervous
and	night sweats that would kill an ox, I can wring out my sheets in the morning; sheets, ha, pun
but	the doctor gives me a clean bill of health, eat less, he says, drink lots of water, write to your local printer, sleep on a hard bed
and	keep your hands on top of the quilt

(h)

but	there's no satisfying women, so why try; the hero; yes, right, by all means, dead on: a quest for a woman who might be satisfied, the holy grail nothing, poor old Who?him gets it into his brief case, he puts out to sea, so to speak, for himself
and	a bird in the hand, he soon discovers, two in ambush, both of them friends, pirating an edition, ha
but	if the fish complain of water
and	when the goat wears a halo, then I too shall be faithful, believe me; a man faithful, a woman satisfied
but	if I am not mistaken, night follows day, cows eat grass

(i)

and	if the shoe fits, wear it, true

but	the poet must resist the poem, if you know what I mean: take, for instance, the woman from Swift Current, she who now loves adverbs
and	I hope she's happy, I'm happy myself
but	you try sitting in this room, sit on your butt, ho, fingers raised like talons
and	say out loud, to yourself, to the window if you prefer: I'm in love
but	I'm over it now, I seldom think of her as anything more than a good, if you'll pardon my saying so, piece
and	that was rather nice, I can honestly say I miss that
but	there's all as well as iota, after as well as before, you know; scratch as well as itch, bite as well as bait, ruin as well as rut, apollonian as well as crazy out of your head
and	I don't blame them for hiking over the hills after a pack of illusions, I'm not a vindictive man

(j)

but	let's pretend that only women suffer
and	that brings to mind a paragon; I mean, she, down there in upstate New York, she who runs after doorknobs
but	thimbles; why thimbles; doorknobs I can see, rocking chairs, trundle beds, dry sinks, fly swatters
and	I might add that more than one woman has said of me, he is, for all his distance, his peccadilloes, his passing infidelities, his inability to boil water, really, the best intentioned of men
but	stop putting words in my mouth, she said, ha
and	yet we do, after all, reason from analogy: is it not a commonplace, for instance, to compare the undulating hills of whatever distant horizon to the breasts of a nearby woman, or vice versa
but	no, you will say, to paragon is elsewhere, let hic be ille
and	yet *The Song of Solomon*, taking the first text that comes to hand, is chockful of just such analogies, heap of wheat: belly; flock of sheep: teeth

but	the woman in Nanaimo, she who lives in a submarine, has, I am told by reliable sources, become enamoured; she is hung up on clams, though why is a mystery to me, I haven't the foggiest

(k)

and	the theory itself fails, the doctrine of, I forget what; not the chain of being, Christ knows, I've tried that one on
but	I can love, even the black holes, even the gaited sun, the galloping night, the earthworm riding the silver grass
and	the bursting guts of this old cinder
but	I'm down today, I'm *don't*
and	take it from me, I am dwarf to her needments, I lug them, after, uphill
but	every cloud has
and	only the surge of blood commends the folly, the belly's worth, the rotund making of round, the reason why monks look hollow, the wind has full cheeks, blow, thou
but	I've sworn off myself
and	a stiff has no conscience

(l)

but	I'll tell you something, I'll let you in on a secret
and	why the ladies haven't guessed my longing, that buffaloes me
but	here goes: throw salt over your left shoulder, avoid cracks, ha, walk away from rather than toward, spell pig backwards
and	say funny
but	I mean: all things being equal, fight fire with fire
and	might not the flame be me, get it; he is a manifestation of I
but	haven't we met
and	might I not be the doorknob too, for whatever earthly reason, the trundle bed, the dial of her phone

but	the woman from Swift Current, putting on airs, avoiding the climb, she knew avoidance
and	there are adverbs, you may remember, of manner, of place, of time; it is possible to be decently alive
but	here
and	now, of course, it isn't fashionable, it isn't done
but	I, The Sad Phoenician of Love, surveying the stars, the old singer, his foot in his mouth, have a right to my opinions

(m)

and	I still think a tree house would have solved all my problems, well, half my problems; peek up her skirt once in a while, sure
but	pull up the ladder or push it away; your kick at the cat, Ludwig
and	she did say something about my being for the birds
but	of course, trust my luck, I wasn't listening, I was hardly conscious, I was, you might say, in seventh heaven, I might have been
and	further, kissing the backs of her knees, climbing, her cheeky ass umbrella, as I climbed, against disaster, Mr. Ladderman, please, she would have said
but	I'm nothing if not honest
and	I wouldn't, except, of course, to please her, raise even my voice
but	it was she who resisted; she, wronged by refusing; life is what we make it they say; maybe even stones have discourse, perhaps there is a music of the spheres, heard on quiet nights, far from water
and	maybe the fireman only climbs to kiss the flame

(n)

but	even if it's true, that my women all have new lovers, offer no pity, remember, the worm turns
and	could it not be argued, the grease gets the squeaking wheel, the bridegroom the bride, the knot gets all or nun, ha, the sea sits firmly on top of land
but	I live by a kind of resistance

and	that explains why I was not there when she hollered uncle, the huntress, she with her glasses strung to her neck, the guide concealed in her canvas purse, a Franklin stove for a mouth, a rocker her hat or hair, two vinegar bottles under her blouse, behind her a round oak table
but	the eye is a liar, the sun does not set
and	any rogue of the first water would know how to wait, time flies, there are other fish in the ocean
but	enough: let one be the square root of one
and	lonely is only lonely, it has no other name like hand or hope or trust, or pissing against the wind, it has no habit of upside-down, it slams no doors, it does not fly south in autumn
but	I love you

(o)

and	if the ladder isn't there when I step off, then he who photographs the wind may find me in the picture, yes
but	give a guy a chance, would you
and	if oops is the right name for accident, then I have come full circle
but	grief has its o too, the ice cream fallen from the cone, the child learning, the orifice of love, open
and	happy the happy oo, as in rue; surprise at the ancient pleasure
but	ouch my ass is dragging
and	that means the end can't be far away, ha; well, all right, I confess: the woman in Montreal, she took up with an old flame
but	you could have warned me, I told her; oh, she said
and	I, the anarchist who needed order, wearing a dandelion at my throat

(p)

but	Miss Reading would look at the fire, not at the light; here's pie on your plate, compose yourself, trala trala
and	I guessed it: the night to her was everything; she could not read it by day, she who bought books

but	only for the torn page: the burning was her alphabet
and	she hurried, sometimes she had not a minute to spare, she praised me, wantonly
but	the mouth gives entrance to exit, kissy-boo

(q)

and	meaning: even in that she found meaning, if not a mime
but	I, The Sad Phoenician of Love, dyeing the world red, dyed laughing, ha, lost everything, lost home; I, homing
and	lost: while she, the children off to school, on the Q.T. whispered: stay away from sunsets, poet, sleep with a window open, on cloudy days take Vitamin C, never trust water
but	track the snail, trick the murex down to red, the last Tyrian purple, worship
and	worship darkly, too; the purple fish, into the round ship, raise; a quaint devouring, this or then
but	nothing matters, I told her; true, she said, so much, so what, you can't get blood from a turnip
and	that's that, I suppose

(r)

but	somewhere today your body is waiting, we rely on the flesh; love is only the consequence, not the cause. Or vice versa. How green, actually, green is.
And	when the dog says grrr, then we are going from bad to burn. Colder than hell, the prairie this morning, frost on the growing grass. The tree house wearing its leafy parka. Yuk.
But	where shall I say you have gone? she said. The poet blew his nose. It's not green, he answered.
And	the submarine too. Inexplicable. Except for the prevalence of same. Even in dark places. See Henry, I beg your pardon, Henri.
But	eat your oysters while you are. Horny contains: a reminding. A regretting. A regressing. A returning. A pretending. A simpering. A forswearing. A slithering. A sundering.

And   the usual remonstrance, of course, double or nothing,
             get hold of yourself
but   no remedy

(s)

and   feeding the beast of her humour, I rampage into my
             own grave, 'sblood
but   still we ask, does the lion dream the sleeper or the
             sleeper the lion
and   s.o.s. says sink or swim; down is out; the cardinal,
             in season only, wears red
but   the plural of would is not, if you see what I mean;
             don't turpentine the dog for chasing a falling star;
             you will, won't you, feed no bears; they lick each
             other's thighs, the lovers
and   a slip of the tongue is never a fault of the mind, ho
but   the venerable poet, wishing to send regrets: I met a
             fellow once, he says, to the friend in Moose Jaw,
             anonymous, practised polygamy; practice makes perfect,
             he claimed
and   a peaceable kingdom

(t)

but   I, naturally enough, was the first man she knew, she
             who loved strawberries next, with cream, then a man
             with a camera for a nose, then adverbs
and   loved them faithfully, all or at once or in turn;
             what fit, fit to a T
but   now she's in love with butterfly eggs, she sits on
             a clutch of broody eggs
and   knits an afghan, asking
but   why is the pain so beautiful, the sky so deep, the
             man in the moon

(u)

and   I'm hardly the same myself, granted
but   stiff-necked women make me uneasy, I'll admit it
             straight out, I'm quiet, I mind my own business

and	the gopher lay down with the hawk, the cabbage plant with the cutworm
but	then, consider, I'm afflicted with common sense, the picture of decency, I, hard-working, dedicated, running over with the milk of whatever, generous even to a fault, gentle with horses
and	with friends resembling the far end of same
but	fair play, that's my motto; I'm first to put out the cat, not one to lie down on the job, except of course, ho; given to elevated thoughts, careful never to slurp soup, surprised by the stains in my clean shorts, a drinker who knows his limits, a whist player of some repute, a lifelong student of Empedocles, the last of a dying breed, embarrassed though not exhausted by too frequent masturbation, a crackerjack at the two-step, unpedantic, slow to anger, a decorous farter, respectful of my elders, even when they haven't got all their marbles
and	a good listener

(v)

but	there are limits, you know: down there in upstate New York, she with a basket on her bench, she posts a sign, garage sale
and	all her Saturday, longing: o button of gold, he loves me not
but	that's another problem, sleep wears me out these days, I wake up tired
and	button of bone, of hoof, of horn, please bury the dead; he loves me not, he loves me not
but	she's barking up the wrong tree
and	button of seed, of shell, o button of linen, button of patent leather; he loves my arms in the sun, he loves the circle of my hair; o button of bronze, of opal, of amber; o button of jade or iron, hoard happiness, honour the past, buy government bonds
but	his, the piratical self, is thief

and   thieving: O button of braid, of brass, she loves me;
            of quartz, of silver, of pewter or wood; O button or
            hole or hook, she loves me now, she loves me; O button
            of celluloid, she loves me not, of sapphire, she loves
            me, of paper, of paste, she loves me not, of
            mother-of-pearl, she loves me, of tin, of polyester,
            tell us the whole truth
but   hide what must be hidden

(w)

and   if the hook fits the eye, madam, whoop-de-doo; the
            old button-plucker, neither does she, nor, having
            done it, say the word; may her first buttonhole be
            her last, the worm gets hungry too, love
but   I remember the taste of sunset, the cargo all below
            deck, the whiff on the sultry air
and   no feasting allowed: the ox, the crane, C as in fig,
            D for door; hieroglyph to no man, he; the horned
            asp
but   don't be embarrassed, we all wear them; G, in outline,
            the camel's head
and   neck, carry on; hanky-pank, all hail; aye, the law
            had the goods on me from the start; ho, skip it, the
            wine bowl empty, no goading at the harried gate
but   dear Miss Reading saw it, the owl, a rising out
            of Montreal; to wit, the city burning, the city,
            burned in the snowing night
and   here in the west she writes me, please, I carried
            the torch for her, ha, could you send one burrowing
            owl, postpaid, I have found a hole in the mountain,
            no more the arctic dream; the Metro, if you don't
            mind
but   he, a fishy business, that, the hooked eye, snitched
            from the nooky night, running his blastfamous poem
            to halt, who goes there, speak
and   ready to call it quits

(x)

but	the woman from Nanaimo, she who lives in a submarine,
	now she is all for shipwrecks, she loves each
	sinking, the bodies caressing the sand, with tongue
and	foot, the clams carouse: deep now she lurks, down;
	shipboards of fir, she announces, to cradle the
	broken sea; a cedar, O Sad Phoenician, to make thee
	a mast
but	keep an ear cocked for sirens, you one-eyed mariner
and	the pole-star pointing you in, fresh from the coast
	of Ampersand, a cargo to Upsilon bound, the calmest
	cove, the engraving sea, hmmm, yummy, the sacker
	said: two of those, please, the big ones
but	wait, don't wrap them, ha

(y)

and	yes, there was, somewhere, a tree, he saw, Who?him
but	you're out of it, the lady said, she was very polite,
	she wore a chair on her head, a basket between her
	knees full of salmon; a butterfly almost the shade
	of a Baltimore oriole licked its perfect proboscis
	to her right nipple: she was the guardian of the
	tree, that was clear
and	the tree itself stood in the distance behind her,
	possibly green, possibly not a tree at all, a sail,
	slumped in the windless air, or only a gallows hung
	with sleep
but	why? Who?him, to the palm that either reached or
	resisted
and	she, a tongue like a wick: whoa, there, horse,
	where's the fire
but	he was as ornery as the day: Pythagoras, he said,
	is the name, playing a long shot; he paused
and	was more than a little disappointed; sir, she said,
	I'll take your word
but	I should tell you, twisting a few of the rings on her
	fingers, you've just, in that case, wiseacre, died
and	she meant it

(z)

but   Who?him didn't know izzard from A, his donkey from
a hole in the ground, aleph or end, he was all gall,
ho; it's a disguise, he ventured

and   that's when the old gal grinned, where the hell you
been, Phoney; she tapped the butterfly tighter, it
was falling down on the job: I know you're slow

but   what took you, if you'll pardon the expression, so
long

and   one more thing, she continued, an egg in her navel
the size of a fist, about your friend, Pythagoras

but   a salmon leapt out of the basket; she caught it,
quick as a flash

and   a bird lit on her bare left shoulder, a long-legged
squawk, out of nowhere: true, it said, swell, okay,
got you, dead on, man, right, we're doing it now,
hang in

but   the tree was not an inch closer. If it was a tree.
The light was too bright for seeing, green became
blue. Or vice versa.

The Silent Poet Sees Red

and	green too, on occasion, granted
but	I wouldn't slander a friend for the world, cross my heart
and	spit to die
but	he shuts off his inboard motor, he sprawls on the deck of his cottage, nursing a beer, he forgets to shave for a week
and	he thinks he's a sailor, Earache the Red; it was he who discovered dry land
but	sit yourself down, he promises, life is short
and	while you're up, crack us a couple of cold ones, poet
but	I hardly have time, he talks too much; he is Professor of Nowhere at some place or other; puck, he says, waving a stick
and	he skates his way through class, defying entropy, slamming the puck under the chairs of his sleeping students
but	women are fooled by his library, ha; he's all show; may he rupture himself, clipping his toenails
and	while I'm on the subject, his wife has four arms, she holds him together, blind as love
but	remember, the pupil is black, we see with darkness only
and	I watch for a light in the west, occidents will happen, ho
but	sunrise comes at noon to her bed
and	what do we have for lunch, breakfast; Silent Poet, she tells me, you are the great keeper, the wellspring of was, the guardian of ought
but	that's your loss, not mine
and	soft as blue she whispers a pip into her palm; west is a colour of the wind

The Silent Poet Moves His Office

but   I can't throw this away

and   the Maalox, god knows I'll need that; some lead for
          a pencil, ha, well

but   the keys; okay, so what if a door does come knocking

and   this paper knife, tarnished almost black, Watzernaym
          left it, open the mail, she said, I send you

but   she must have forgot

and   the English penny that didn't bring luck

but   Earache the Red appears in my doorway, gives me the
          willies; ho, he says, caught you

and   I'm guilty, I blush; surreptitiously I check my
          fly; saw the boxes out in the hall

but   what, he adds, exactly, is the function of objects,
          if you don't mind my asking

and   he answers, waving a book, this yours by any chance

but   I'm holding a packet of papers, the band breaks,
          the rubber is old

and   I pick up a letter, from a patient in the asylum;
          you love me, she says, I can tell by your poems; the
          broken draft of her address, there in the corner; I
          was going to scrawl her a note, a quick apology
          even, maybe send her something

but   I open the Maalox

and   Earache the Red is shouting, the blur in his hand a
          mousetrap, the blood confused me, in the wire frame,
          the staring eyes; we transfer memory, he
          predicates; more easily put, we chicken

but   I take the book, words that I've never seen before,
          underlined by my assertion

and   Earache the Red is raving, the object is, he says,
          not to object, get it; he peeks out into the hall;
          he farts

but   consider, picking up three sticks of chalk; he
          points; consider this ruler you've carried with
          you, from boyhood on; this embarrassing print of
          a rapids you never hang, this tape you haven't the
          courage to hear; consider, my friend; he points;
          this homemade valentine, this pair of scissors,
          this rock

and	I think to myself, I'm sorry, forgive me, I didn't mean it
but	I go down the hall, my wrists in pain, carrying everything

The Silent Poet at Intermission

but	who are all these strangers, I ask
and	I mean it, heading for the bar
but	trust my luck, Earache the Red, a drink in either hand, announces, Madame Sosostris has a bad cold this evening, we laugh
and	I say, that's pharaoh enough
but	nobody gets it, I buy my own
and	Earache, the crowd gathering, art should instruct, he tells us, glancing at his own reflection
but	not by painting the rainbow black, we laugh
and	I have a pot myself, Labatt's did that much for me
but	she who loves gold loves elsewhere
and	follows the path prophesying no end, it's hardly hard to guess; uppie uppie, she says in the morning, the medium well done
but	he hands her a glass, she looks; here's mud in your eye
and	even the Virgin Queen, she wasn't Shakespeare either
But	I did scorn them all, she wrote
and	with good cause: a leman is a lemon, ha; well, let the heads fall
but	music, he says, is the mothering lode; he waves his arms; he is composing a series of dichotomies for violin
and	fiddle, the chiselling clod
but	he spills his drink
and	I wipe my shoe on my cuff; I hear the weasel that sniffs the hen, the blood-loud blood in the gutter, the wise man strangling on his own; sorry, mum
but	he discovers, just then, the split of mind
and	body; putting Descartes before the hearse, we laugh
but	just as I raise the dagger the buzzer sounds, I am left with the thought in my hand

and	he takes her elbow in his palm; the news, he tells us, straight to our backs, must learn to be old, to learn to be new; we scratch ourselves
but	follow, as we lead, to the first usher
and	I leave for home, bumping knees with a dozen strangers
but	never go

The Silent Poet Finds Out

and	they'll get me, I know, dread or alive
but	I go out at night, with my shovel, I dig deep holes in the neighbours' lawns
and	Earache the Red, at coffee, for god's sake hit the sack early, he says, you look like you never sleep
but	watch those dirty dreams; he winks
and	shakes his spoon in my direction
but	I don't let on that I understand
and	the mayor is offering a reward, some maniac, he claims, dug a toilet pit, directly in front of City Hall; the reward is an insult, I'm worth more
but	I look at the posters, I'm tempted, poets are not well paid, I could use the money
and	the grave in the bishop's garden, I don't think that was mine, I never dig graves
but	isn't that the truth, they see what they believe, people, I go out at night, I dig deep holes
and	a friend, late for a meeting, fell headlong into a gap in the campus green
but	didn't smile
and	I was alone again in the world
but	Earache, there's a new law, he says, you're legally responsible for all your dreams
and	I buy his coffee
but	just last night, while he snored in her arms, I pitched black dirt at his window
and	walled him in
but	he doesn't let on; he calls for a refill; I'm sweating
and	he looks at the morning paper, then looks at me; in China they've picked up a signal, I wait

but	he takes three sugars, I hate that about him; quick energy, he says; he winks
and	I hide my blisters under the table

The Silent Poet Craves Immortality

and	even black has its lighter moments, ha
but	the doggerel of the sun is such, we stare blankly
and	I stop criticizing my friends, I praise their ugly faces, their staggering poems
but	they agree
and	then I wonder at my own judgement; I nod; they slap my back, you've mellowed
but	that makes it worse, I watch TV
and	memorize the weather, promising, first thing in the morning, I'll write the last line
but	secretly at night I turn signs around, I point all travellers in the wrong direction; I've so far derailed three trains; I look at bridges malignantly
and	pray with the first two fingers of each hand crossed
but	she, in the bathroom, washing between her legs, what are you doing on your knees
and	I leap up
but	I think I'm preparing to die, I can smell food inside a closed fridge, the milk a little sour, the onions gone soft, as in a wet garden, the hamburger practising green
and	I bought new dishes yesterday, bright plates, Italian, flowers on a white background, six Japanese bowls, I can taste the roses
but	cheap, something you could stack in a tomb, send out on the water
and	Jezebel, she sees I'm reading in bed, I study maps, this is Alberta, I look for rivers that trail off into dotted lines, this is the Yucatan, this the Siberian forest; I peruse a linguistic atlas, looking for one word
but	she knows I'm watching; she lifts a foot into the basin, slow as sin
and	I put in a bid for a ship, a rust-eaten tanker, nothing pretentious

but	something, nevertheless, that will burn with a flare, ho
and	give a signature to the sky

The Silent Poet Eats His Words

but	whatever you do, don't
and	remember, forget what I said about Watzernaym, miss or hit, she didn't love me
but	not in the way I wanted not to be loved, I've had enough
and	that's only a start, she was an admirer of bricks, she liked their fired faces, their false
but	predictable ends
and	darkness itself she would nothing
but	praise, it falls, she said, not like you, feigning a light
and	I learned to hate from her loving, her ink pot, calling the letter back; I teased her awake
but	touch your typewriter, poet, she whispered, then I can sleep in the morning
and	that was a hard one to swallow, ho; I tried for an hour
but	life is a series, I explained, I drew diagrams on the frosted window, I brushed the wrinkles from the sheet where I wanted her to lie
and	after another failure I stood, delicately, on my own head, defying her to tell up from down; love, I said, I'm inclined to agree
but	the penny saved is, generally, lost; a stitch in time seams nothing, ha
and	I argued, at length, for the inevitable rise of the real, into Idea; this time it's forever, I added
but	all my blood sank to my brain, I was left hanging, my neck hurt; I was trying to amuse
and	Ahab, I said, was a fool to marry you, Jezebel
but	don't feel bad, I'm depressed myself, there's a flock of two thousand birds that shits on my car, they sit in this saskatoon bush, see, waiting
and	when I drive up the leader says, shit
but	sometimes I fool them; I hesitate; just as I open the door

and	after they've all obeyed the command, like the stooges they are, I step out, regally, majestically, I step from the car, I bow, just slightly; Francis, I say, is the name; skip the saint business
but	she was sound asleep, except for a rhythmic snoring, suggesting she might be awake; please, she said, jerking the covers from the place where I might have been, read the review of your book again, make some coffee, scrub that goddamn kitchen floor, vacuum, take your pulse, fix the toaster, go put on your snow tires, asshole, it's January

The Winnipeg Zoo

yes, I am here, exhausted, a wreck, unable
to imagine the act of writing, unable to imagine

I am here, it is quiet, I am exhausted from
moving, we must take care of our stories

the moving is a story, we must take care, I am
here, I shall arrive, I am arriving, I too

have waited, the way in is merely the way,
she takes her lovers, reader, listen, be careful

she takes her lovers one by one to the Winnipeg
zoo, she winds her hair on her fingers, the hook

in the ceiling holds the plant, the ivy climbs
to the floor, must is the end

of winter, the ride to the zoo, the sun on the
man at the gate, the hair wound on her fingers

she takes her lovers, first, the startled boy
stares at the pink flamingos, they rest, folding

one leg at a time, the standing boy, she returns
alone from the Winnipeg zoo, her brown eyes

misting into calm, the hook in the ceiling
holds the plant, what matters is all that matters

the man at the gate says nothing, the kiss of
the Canada lynx, the lightning touch of the snake

is hot, love is round, thumbs are still fingers,
we must take care of our stories, the reptiles

waiting, do not move, flamingos have no names,
the boy, the tall young man, reaching to find her

hand, the polar bear dives deep, into the coiling
water, Audubon raises his gun, the artist

the owl is master of sleep, don't follow,
she takes her lovers past the pond

the farmer from Delacroix, the one who grows
asparagus spears, the one who feeds gourmands

is watching the reptiles, he does not move,
we must take care of our stories, or what it is

is only this, thumbs are still fingers, always,
after an early lunch, the zoological garden

the secret is in the ketchup bottle, the farmer
has short toes, red hair, he wears blue shoes

the man at the gate is not counting, a trickle of
gold at her neck, no wind, her scattered love

is round, Audubon raises his gun, the cranes
reply to the wild turkeys, always, after

an early lunch, the farmer, his hands to the glass,
it is quiet, reader, listen, she comes back alone

flamingos have no names, monkeys learn by hanging,
the lawyer, cracking sunflower seeds, spits

at the watching tiger, he reaches to take
her hand, the popcorn vendor winks

at a scalding baby, somewhere, rococo,
a killdeer furrows the air, the lawyer

cracking sunflower seeds, spits at the tiger's
yellow eyes, but cannot quite imagine

the artist, Audubon, dipping the beaded sight
into the flattened v on the gun's barrel, we must

take care, the sun is a fish,
monkeys learn by hanging, the lizard is only

half asleep, write on the post card, quickly,
I am here, yes, I want to go home, the man

at the gate is not counting, Audubon dips the
beaded sight into the flattened v on the gun's

barrel, the lawyer, cracking sunflower seeds,
the tiger blinks, politely, I am here

exhausted, she is with me, the artist,
Audubon, tightens his index finger

her eyes mist into a calm, the elk
in the distant pasture raises his rack

then it is done, the ducks in the duck pond
cannot fly, the sun sticks out its shadow

we must take care of our stories, I am ex—
hausted from moving, it is quiet, I am here

1.

A lemon is almost round.
Some lemons are almost round.
A lemon is not round.

So much for that.

How can one argue that a lemon
is truly a lemon,
if the question can be argued?

So much for that.

I said, to Smaro
(I was working on this poem),
Smaro, I called, is there
(she was in the kitchen)
a lemon in the fridge?
No, she said.

So much for that.

2.

As my father used to say,
well I'll be cow-kicked
by a mule.

He was especially fond of
lemon meringue pie.

3.

I went and looked at Francis Ponge's poem
on blackberries. If blackberries can be
blackberries, I reasoned, by a kind of analogy,
lemons can, I would suppose, be lemons.

Such was not the case.

4.

Sketches, I reminded myself,
not of a pear,
nor of an apple,
nor of a peach,
nor of a banana
(though the colour
raises questions),
nor of a nectarine,
nor, for that matter,
of a pomegranate,
nor of three cherries,
their stems joined,
nor of a plum,
nor of an apricot,
nor of the usual
bunch of grapes,
fresh from the vine,
just harvested,
glistening with dew—

Smaro, I called,
I'm hungry.

5.

What about oranges?
At least an orange
looks like an orange.
In fact, most oranges
bear a remarkable resemblance
to oranges.

6.

Smaro is rolling a lemon on the breadboard.
The breadboard, flat, horizontal, is motionless.
The lemon rolls back and forth on the motionless surface.
Smaro's hand moves horizontally, back and forth,
over the rolling lemon.

One could draw a diagram of the three related objects,
deduce therefrom a number of mechanical principles.

7.

I had a very strong desire
to kiss a lemon.
No one was watching.
I kissed a lemon.

So much for that.

8.

I bought a second-hand car—
Okay, okay.

9.

If someone asked me,
how is a lemon shaped?

        (the salmon
        (the oven
        (the lemon

I'd say a lemon is shaped
exactly like an hour.

(Now we're getting somewhere.)

  10.

The lemon cure.
In each glass
mix: 1 stick cinnamon
        1 teaspoon honey
        2 cloves
        2 jiggers rum
        1/2 slice lemon
        hot water to taste

Repeat as necessary.

11.

poem for a child who has just bit into
a halved lemon that has just been squeezed:

    see, what did I tell you, see,
    what did I tell you, see, what
    did I tell you, see, what did
    I tell you, see, what did I
    tell you, see, what did I tell
    you, see, what did I tell you,
    see, what did I tell you, see,
    what did I tell you, see, what
    did I tell you, see, what did
    I tell you, see, what did I
    tell you, see, what did I tell
    you, see, what did I tell you

One could, of course, go on.

12.

This hour is shaped like
a lemon.   We taste its light

on the baked salmon.
The tree itself is elsewhere.

We make faces, liking the
sour surprise. Our teeth melt.

The Criminal Intensities of
Love as Paradise

Morning, Jasper Park

etymologies
of sun or
stone of ear
and listening

the bent of
birth on edge
the chrysalis
and parting bone

old as old as
time as time   *hearing*
holding   *footfalls*
hand of hand   *that must*
                                be those
& ripe as rite   *of a bear*
the dreamers
dreaming
feet or foot

of lodgepole &
a bear below   *the lovers*
bellow   *awake*
a nose   *in their*
                                tent
jay song   *in the*
and scolding   *forest*
timpani to
skald of scene

the once upon
the figurine
of eye
insinuating

the is of light
is all or all
the ending of
the lip on lip

Fire & Pan

similitude
of fire waits
as always as
a waltz

this stopping of
must now go on
an axe to axiom
or folded arm

cripes a killed   *the lovers*
god or still
the scanning ear
astray or astral

or nickelodeon   *debating*
of beast & bird   *who shall*
a thrust of thumb   *remain in the*
cretaceous   *sleeping bag*
                                   who
in eiderdown the   *crawl out*
labyrinth of belly   *to kindle*
beg or theseus   *a fire*
& bully too

the luting pan
unscramble skull
or chipmunk
wittgenstein

as wind is
metaphysical   *quarrel*
a tree so slowly
lays its eggs

lovers have hold
of hold and
turn and turn
the flapjack mind

Breakfast, After, & Looking

                                      in which
                                      the lovers

                                      leaving their
                                      breakfast dishes
                                      to soak in a
or even elk   *yellow plastic*
in elk meadow   *pail*
or forest
allowing tree   *walk towards*
                                      the distant
hello & hollow   *falls*
how
the knocking knuckle
knocks

perfect as
spoon or pillow
was or would or
willow bunch

the bell
ringing the bell
the cryptic message
in the scar

profanely lucid
fall or hail
the mountain
all alone alone

ride or riddance
to the last field
radiance of
washed rock

risking the
loud fever
roses and red
& violets

to make a song
to make a song
the folding water
feed the eye

Standing near a Waterfall

the torque of
absolute desire
river & the wind
arouse

as rounded as
a hat the head
so quickly now
and o so clean

or wind or wind
of memorizing
dark the drop
of spanking stone

bent & the break
and then comes
after after
the reaching sea

the lunar patterns
of the mind
and horse beware
the horse

as fetal as
precambrian
or harlequin to
stopped throat

or yet the hand
unarmed unharmed
return
& cinquefoil bloom

or fountain wild
of jack & jill
the maelstrom of
and columbine

o this is where
the raven fell
& this is where
the raven fell

*there being
a ledge handy
the lovers
standing
upon it
consider
the usual
lovers' leap*

Salt, of Ocean Sea, of Tears

the forfeiture
of ending
to begin begin
& arch & heel

the tent's hot
light
or flagging or
the caved eye

the finding hand
or mouthing &
the salted sea
open and trade

a new america
pepper & tears
or heraclitus if
skulduggery

the darting of
& tongue & tongue
sheet or heat of
lightning

cry out & cry
white
as alabaster is
or dipping gull

to god or after
and a portraiture
of merely is
or queen of spain

*having
narrowly
avoided
death*

*the lovers
return to
their tent
intending
to have*

a quickie

Awoken and, Again, Hungry, Again

& death as proud
as death
or harping amphion
arouse a wall

the lovers
while eating
a bologna sandwich
and drinking
the first beer
of the day
hold discourse
as to which

ankle or calf
annihilate
the back of knee
recite racine

of all their
zones
is most
erogenous

or moose rutting
or mossy ear
the atavistic
buttock bare

becoming of
of teeth
to peeled root
or onion even

but belly
button best
lending
& all directions

Into Town

whole wheat or
rye or 2%
or skim
riddle the take

or taco stand
arise arise
& soft ice cream
& zero meet

and then
the lovers
decide that

or zeno
one white lie
tucking to heart
the arrow's nib

instead of
driving up to
the columbia
icefields to

the bandit tree
or ashtray sign
decorum and its
data cross

spend the day
taking pictures
or maybe hiking
they'll zip
into town

on floor on
floor or mall
or siwash
melt the feet

for a loaf
of bread and
some milk
and maybe
even a

far & the rattle
meet the bear &
norse nor apple
plastic head

jug of
donini

Postcard to a Hillside

sunwapta &
or athabasca
or the sliding
in interior

a postcard to
the raven's beak
and lovers' eyes
are taller now

the lovers
stop
to look
at the

antipodes of
everywhere
explode the
book of hours

totem pole
by the
CN tracks

& postcard to
a poet's name
unhook to learn
the rainbow fish

or postcard then
to dead
vivaldi
play o play o play

& of & to mt robson
p s hi
where rivers braid
the gelded sand

Nude Swimmers in Late Afternoon

& alpha &
a road allowance
& red squirrel
paying crow

guide & end
to nowhere   *mosquitoes*
lost pool &   *be damned*
jaybird white
                                    the lovers
waiting & fare   *pull off the*
warning or way   *road and*
blue water &   *likewise*
a wry step   *pull off their*
                                    clothes and
& scree & cliff   *go for a*
montane   *swim*
pubic as   *in the buff*
periphery & ah

the ha the hoo
mounting and
dip and deep
hullabalooing

shivering

huh & the hee
hieratic
& holy old
& jumping

the plash
and kiss and
wrought hands
roughing

and fescue
grass &
offering
& myriad tongue

Campsite, Home, Away From

or tree as roof
and origin
and savaging
the height of hill

& the lost & the
late home always
found
in the small flame

lovers are only
this and more
a cracking stick
a mortal sun

or fish or bird
or beast
and a black pot
and fire fending

*smoke rising
from numerous
fires*

the icon element
the scalp
reminding   *children*
cheese & wine   *at play*

and barking at
a dog a dog   *the camp*
or venus maybe   *busy*
or baked beans

                                             and campers
                                             asking
                                             each other
                                             where
                                             they are
                                             from

Bear Story with or without Bear

& the knick-knack
day done &   *the lovers*
night & night   *turn off*
or a pocket moon   *the coleman*
                                             lantern
& after the least   *and then*
page or last   *quickly*
coals fanned   *crawl into*
passage & end   *the sack*

or tent flap &   *and lie awake*
the forecast low
forest & fain
& would lie down

                                             listening
rank as the rank
scenting of bear
bear baiting
breath

catching & bruit
enactment
far or fury
wizarding fear

and in the arms
and arms of and
a creature or
o creaking wind

both & both &
drifting to
or holding
lapidary dark

wisp of the
toldtale
midnight
teller & arrive

And Dreamers, Even Then, if Dreaming

over the chained
mountain
the ridebound eagle
risk & tame

& hover the long
wings waived
& wide as wide
as sleep

eerie & enter   *and now*
if   *the lovers*
& the pale garden   *find*
chill as white   *the perfect*
                          glacier
                          of all
or stalled in   *their*
draglong and   *once*
the pitchfall   *ambitions*
slide

the storm
commencing speed
the spider
reach

albino night
to extricate
the called
grammarian

the closed eye
listen &
o nesting tongue
hatch the world

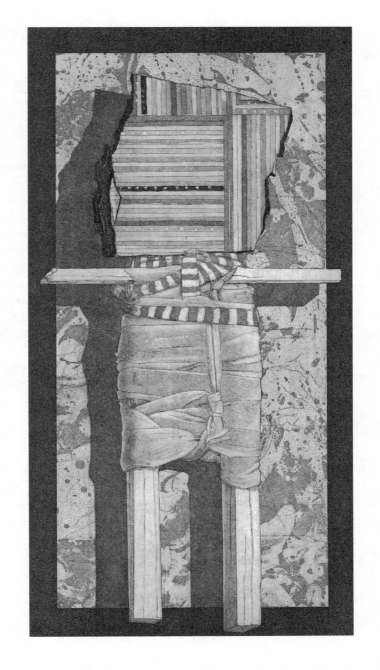

II — ADVICE TO MY FRIENDS

Advice to My Friends

1. For a Poet Who Has Stopped Writing

if we could just get a hold of it,
catch aholt, some kind of a line,
if the sun was a tennis ball or something
but it ain't, the impossible thing is the sun

if words rhymed, even, we could catch a holt
(a bush) and start the stacking, words
lined up, I mean, like, in the old days
wood behind the kitchen stove

but you take now your piecemeal sonnet
wow, certain of these here poets,
these chokermen can't even count to fourteen
and as for Petrarch, well, I mean

I've been to bed with some dandy and also skilled
ladies, sure, but would I a ballyhoo start
for the keen (and gossipy) public?
I'd be sued or whatever, maybe killed

but (now and then) you've got to tell *some*body
and a reader has I guess, in spite of all, ears

2.   *To Eli Mandel, Setting His New Alarm*

time was elapsing, sure, but when does it not
and always elapse?
and hauling out, we were, the logos
from the forest of earthly delights

you and Dennis, Smaro and I, holus-bolus
drinking wine at the dining-room table,
Eli: night, you were trying to set your new alarm
the birthday gift, the gift from Ann

what time is it now? you asked, gave us a fright
Dennis raising the spectre of the stove's handy clock
over the books of poems, Ritsos, Suknaski, Pound, Webb
we were reading aloud to each other

and by the time you had let spin by
the digital flash of LOCK, of ALARM
it wasn't that time, time passes, will, amen
what time is it *now*? you, wantonly, asked

and, like the guy said, if you really think
you can get away with it, thank again

3.   To the Wahs, on the Kootenay River

Lao Tzu was right about these matters.
I forget what he said—the way concealed
in its namelessness, or something like it.
Anyways, one by one we climbed the stairs

to visit your newest bathroom, under,
as they say, construction, up on the roof
of your old house. Even the Queen must pause,
allow a smile, apprehending the throne.

Need is an insufficient cause. Laughter
has other fears. We climbed the starlit stairs
where Fred and his brother, having opened
the roof, let out the bottom of affairs.

Twinned in the higher darkness, not with stars
but with the plumbing, I heard myself call
down to my own absence, Where's the light switch?

Poet, a voice replied. Let the chips fall.
Think of yourself there as your own shadow.
Consider submission. Forget desire.

4.   *Slocan Valley, July 17, 1983: For Smaro*

while we together were *swyving*, here
this mountain afternoon, in the late light
on the floor of your study, ravens called
in the all around of this high log mansion

snow on the farthest mountain melted
there in what seems the west but cannot be
unless the sun this morning, as unscheduled as we
rose in the north, while we did *swyve*

a hummingbird alone, out in the sun-deck light
at the hanged feeder, found its unlikely bill
into the jewel-red nectar (those birds so tuned
to fly backwards, alert to surprise from behind)

while even you, blind to the quaint wings
that made that sound (and, making, held
hot the mountains to the rearing sky!)

asked if I had remembered to, or would,
or ever will, the bottle of white wine
in the fridge, put, to chill

5.   *Listening to the Radio: For Michael Ondaatje*

Morenz makes a breakaway down the ice.
He fakes to the left; he draws out the goalie.
He stops. He blushes and says, to all
of the Montreal Forum: Emily Carr, I love you.

Everyone is surprised. The puck delays
the stick, only the ice moves. The (almost)
invisible moment, before he (Morenz) shoots.
The goalie's mask in the goal's mouth.

The splendid rigour of his pads. Not the puck
in the net but the goalie's mask, moving
and stopping. Emily thinks of berry-picking.
She wants to sit in the penalty box.

If you eat the berries, she thinks, the pail
will never fill. Pay attention to the play,
Howie, she whispers, across the blue line.

Everyone is surprised. She blushes and says,
The wedding will be divided into three periods
of twenty minutes each. Morenz shoots.

6. *Reading It in the (Comic) Papers: For bp*

In a delightful ceremony at the bride's
boarding house in Victoria, the nuptial
event is consummated. The family
of Mr. Morenz is not in attendance.

Among the highlights of the afternoon
is the arrival of the poet bpNichol of Toronto
in the company of a Mr. Basho of Japan,
the latter using a hockey stick as his staff.

Work on your line, bp quips (he is wearing
his Buddha shirt) when introduced to the
famous hockey player by Miss Carr (who will retain
her maiden name). Keep it edgy,

Mr. Morenz replies, scoring a point
of his own while he takes the hockey stick
from Mr. Basho's hand–that same Mr. Basho
offering, in his now empty hands, his gift:

When we both talk, Mr. Basho says, speaking
to all those present, the words are listening.

At the wedding reception, such as it is,
Howie Morenz is asked to say a few words.
He is about to oblige when a menagerist
enters the parlour, accompanied by thirteen

ghazals. I thought ghazals were animals,
Howie says, into the microphone. He gives himself
a body check. He doesn't much like the wedding cake,
he's having a slice of Limburger cheese with onion.

Howie feels about Limburger cheese the way Emily
feels about monkeys. A matter of parallel lines
that meet. The mathematics of (pure) desire.
The hockey player, the artist: they both have

strong wrists. Perhaps, says Emily, the salmon,
coming back, wish to climb the totem tree, or
time is the monkey, descending. Or, Mr. Basho
continues, it is simply a matter of setting out

when you are old. He walks across the parlour
and mingles with the ghazals. Howie takes a bow.

8. *Wedding Dance, Country-Style*

This will not be, Mr. Ondaatje explains,
your standard epithalamium. He is taking
pictures, both in colour and black and white.
The bride and the bridegroom are dancing.

Actually, everyone is dancing. George
(which George?) is dancing, with Gertrude Stein.
All of Victoria, later, expresses embarrassment,
but the dance, the dance is full of marvels.

Roy Kiyooka arrives by balloon. He drops in
for a polka. He is the only person who brings
an escape plan as a gift. It is a collage
of 1,243 pages, in code, with maps and diagrams,

all of which Mr. Ondaatje photographs
as part of the epithalamium, and the ecstatic
document, in arrest, has about it the air

of a painting of a forest exploding into light,
or of a hockey game, under the lights, exploding.
But the dance, the dance is the first decoding.

The shivaree is pronounced a success,
taking place as it does near the family home
of the bridegroom; the assembled neighbours,
who start the evening in disgruntlement, sing

the couple's praise, then eat pancakes at dawn,
with maple syrup, to the music of gun and kettle,
thanks to the magical red cape and skills
theatrical of Mr. Thompson, an oldish young man

who as a boy in southwestern Ontario played road
hockey with Howie Morenz, the two of them (players)
knocking frozen horse turds up and down an otherwise
quiet street and, in the process, recognizing

as had the bride, Miss Carr, earlier, while being
violently seasick in a small boat that was
(supposedly) carrying her to a site where she might
make sketches and, fortunately, sit reasonably still

that the cabbage, folding itself, unfolds, or
as Mr. Thompson put it: nothing is faster than ice.

10.   Back in the Spring of '76: For Laurie Ricou

Let the surprise surprise you, I said
(or should have), follow the pencil's
disregard, even if other ideas mutter.
The wind in Lethbridge has it own gee

and haw. Butter melts in the sun. Rejoice.
The Hutterite men come into town on
Thursdays only (more or less), to try a
barley sandwich; their wives and daughters buy

bolts of bright cotton. Earth rides the air.
Ducks in the irrigation ditches quack
where rotten leaves unhitch to rising waters.
Merchants unpack new merchandise.

I tried aloud "Seed Catalogue"; I bent
your ear. And you, filling my glass, then yours,
asked if chinooks gave me a fever.

The Hutterite men at the next table
nodded. Their tired eyes had farmed the wind.
You're in the seed business? a boss inquired.

11. Laurie Ricou Waiting to Present a Paper Entitled
     "The Intersections of Plain/s Space and Poetry,"
     March, 1982

Should we have another beer? you said,
there in that bar in Lincoln, Laurie;
we were drinking Coors, Cliff's Lounge,
12th St. and O, under an elegant smoke shop

and the cabbie, dropping us off: this bar
is owned by the governor's (he closed one
eye) kid brother, their names ain't spelled
exactly the same, but don't be fooled

and we weren't, or were, on the bald-headed plains,
down in a basement bar, under an elegant
smoke shop, a waitress filling our popcorn bowl
as fast as we scooped it empty

outside two streets intersecting, one of them
numbered, the other wearing the alphabet
itself, the brother of the governor of the Great
State of Nebraska quite possibly in charge:

Should we have another beer? you said, checking
your watch, looking around at the empty chairs.

12. *Late Fall Drive: For Byrna Barclay*

I find the mountains pretentious today.
Early yesterday, driving west alone
across the prairies, I thought of swinging
south off Number One to visit shortgrass

country. Down there, everything is real,
even the emptiness. The buttes are bare.
Trees are only a memory. But I decided not to
go, mostly because a woman in a parka,

pumping gas just outside Moose Jaw, asked
where I was going. South, I said. And she,
checking the oil: There's nothing there to see,
but it's really pretty. She cleaned my windshield.

She would only stand by the roadside, measuring
space by her stillness. She didn't wave
when I left. She wasn't trying to please.

Driving into the mountains now, I notice scars
on the aspen; elk, one hard winter here
in these purple mountains, ate bark off the trees.

13. *November 9, 1983: For Robert Hilles*

Just what the hell is a nature poem,
Robert? Here I am in Calgary to talk
a reading, six hours early, thanks (a lot)
to Air Canada's schedule. I have, in

the Holiday Inn on 8th, a room where
I could write a poem or have (or not) a
sexual fantasy, but instead I walk
the slick sidewalks, watching the snow

come down. It's hardly even snow. Well,
yes, it's snow all right, white enough.
The small flakes blur the tall buildings,
their walls reflect, you guessed it,

snow. Snow is the text, read it, poet.
Fat chance. The air is full
of musical notes. White notes, that is.
They melt to grey on my glasses. I can

hardly read. The sidewalk is slick.
The molten towers, high on the season's
first snow, sway around me. I'm almost
shy. But then I begin to join the dance.

14. *I Find Myself Reading the Old Guys Now: December 6, 1983*

They knew it all, those guys: *First did I fear,*
when first my love began, Giles Fletcher wrote
when love first got him by the throat to guide
his hand, or rock his boat; ship and moon sail

in all those poems; love is a mote or
two of dust in the eye of the boater,
I thought; but now at sea and tempest-tost
I read the books an old-time sorrow wrought:

Fair is my love and cruel as she's fair,
Sam Daniel said, and promptly sailed himself
into his dear love's deep and dang'rous bed
as I have done, somehow confusing port

and storm: you say it's over now and, click,
here I am, clinging to the moon, seasick.

having sworn to reach the Indies,
having persuaded the King and Queen to pay
  at least part of the shot,
having got hold of three ships
  (the *Pinta*, the *Niña*, the *Santa María*),
having embarked,
having met in the Canaries
  a beautiful widow, and fallen in love,
  and left in the name of duty,
having promised the men that,
  in two days, with no land sighted,
  we will turn toward home,
having crossed the wide ocean sea,
having come to this ragged island
  where bodies run naked down to the beach
  to embrace our arrival,

  we swear we have found what we sought.
  What might we say otherwise?

16. Seeing the Bear

In my dream I'm running
toward the bear. I have no choice.
The night is black but
the bear is blacker than the night,
I run toward the bear,
hollering. Smaro awakens me
out of my muffled cries, my trembling.
Did you see the bear too? I ask her.

Smaro begins to laugh, she laughs,
repeating my question. At last,
I tell her, I have begun the poem
of my country, you are present
at the moment of conception,
I wish that John Cabot could be with us,
and Champlain, and maybe Susanna Moodie,
here in our bed, in Winnipeg.

You were right, Columbus,
to try and trick us,

                The Americas are not

    here, the gold of the Inca gods
    has not been stolen,
    the fish of the Grand Banks
    still swim, inviolate and thick,
    in the cold green water,
    the forests of Lake Erie
    ring loud with calling birds,
    the buffalo of the Great Plains
    graze in their millions,
    the wide whales, splendiferous and fat,
    sing their way
    through the Inland Passage,
    the salmon leap totemic
    over coastal villages.

Thief and liar, Columbus,
you taught us everything
we know. What a pity Amerigo

Vespucci pulled that fast one,
got the illusion named
after himself.

18. Four Questions for George Bowering

Michelin Green Guide: "The University [of Bologna], founded in
11C, had 10,000 students in 13C. At that time the professors were
often women and a solemn chronicler reports that one of them,
Novella d'Andrea, was so beautiful in face and body that she had to
give her lectures from behind a curtain to avoid distracting her
pupils."

You who wrote *Kerrisdale Elegies*,
tell me:

Does the body teach us nothing?
What is it that we seek to learn
instead of beauty?
What do they mean, "distracting her pupils"?

I too once lectured in Bologna.
It was February, the room was cold,
I was more than adequately dressed.
No one put up a curtain.

What would happen if, just as you
slid into home plate,
the pitcher threw the catcher
an orange?

19. *Stairway: For Giovanna Capone*

About your grandfather, there, outside Bologna,
growing grapes, making wine, letting
the deep red wine ferment
two cellars down below his kitchen,

bringing the finest bottles up
one stone step each evening,
letting no change of altitude
unsettle the years' aging—

I like to imagine, not the taste of the wine,
but the old man's evening descent,

the tips of his fingers touching each
bottle, lifting it, setting it one step higher,

the way he catches his breath, lets out a
sigh, the day's task
                    accomplished.

20. *A Ritual for One*

having got up to take two Tylenol tablets
     and to look out the window,
having gone back to bed with
     the light on in the bathroom,
having neither slept nor not slept,
having crossed the Sahara in a single night,
     without a camel, and me not believing
     in dreams,
having radioed for help
     on a dead radio,
having checked to see if
     the telephone is working,
having come to this longing
     for the familiar, this
     ancient longing,
     in a strange world

I sit at the breakfast table this morning,
enjoying a cup of coffee.

"... hockey is a *transition game*: offence to
defence, defence to offence, one team to another.
Hundreds of tiny fragments of action, some leading
somewhere, most going nowhere. Only one thing is
clear. Grand designs don't work."

—Ken Dryden, *The Game*

:   being some account of a journey through
western Canada in the dead of six nights

I.

I looked at the dust
on the police car hood.
I looked around the horizon.
(Insert here passage on
nature—

try: The sun was blight
enough for the wild rose.
A musky flavour on the milk
foretold the cracked earth ...

try: One crow foresaw my fright,
leaned out of the scalding
air, and ate a grasshopper's
warning ...

try: A whirlwind of gulls
burned the black field white,
burned white the dark ploughman
and the coming night ...)

←────────────────────────────

I AM A SIMPLE POET
I wrote in the dust
on the police car hood.

Chateau (A Landing) Frontenac

crisp, and the wind
the winter bleat

rain and the best
are never mulled

champlain
is green

madonna
the river is hungry

champlain, look in
my window, wait

absurd as undertow
or word

the hurt of lovers
hand in hand

repay the rot
the risk, the rain

madonna
madrona

announce and
enter, adding (end)

champlain is green
has empty eyes

westering is
madrona, west

the wooden shore
to look inland

2.

Where did the virgin come from
on my second night west?

> Let me, prosaically, parenthetically, remark
> from what I observed: the lady in question took
> from the left (or was it right?) pocket of her
> coffee-stained apron a small square pad of lined
> sheets of paper. She bit the wood back from
> the lead of a stub of pencil. And she wrote,

←——————————————————————————————————

> without once stopping to think, the loveliest
> goddamned (I had gauged her breasts when she
> wiped the table) poem that Christ ever read.

She had a clean mind.

Driving, Accidental, West

1.

the shaped infinity
to hammer home

help, and the wild geese
heading south

and every way and
which, confuse

the fall of light
the fatal peen

how, and the commonest
crow or sparrow

speak the pale
or sensing moon

2.

accelerate, the swan
sing, or eloquent as

antelope, the crisp
rejoinder of the duck's

quack to the deer's
leap, and, even then

even, a static dream
twitter and acquit

the kill, wait, for
and the nasty snow

fall, fall and for
tonight, only, dream

3.

On the third night west
a mountain stopped us.
The mountains were lined up
to dance. I raised my baton:
rooted in earth, the lightning
rod on the roof of the barn,
on my soul's body. A crow
flew over the moon. I raised
my baton, a moon, a mountain.

*

⟵

The crow flew over the mountain

─────────────

*I have removed from this stanza the two lines

Verily, I insist: I did
not raise the purple crow

(and I like the ambiguity created by the line break)

partly because the "Verily" intrudes what we might call another
language code, and that an unfortunate one in this case, for all the
play on *truth*;

partly because the sexual innuendo puts me, as actual poet behind
the implied speaker ("I") in a bad light; that is, self-mockery is, so
to speak, harder to come by, as one (the poet, the implied speaker,
the I or the "I") grows older (RK).

Descent, as Usual, into Hell

i've told her now so long
so often and sojourn *salut*

diamond
star or

(*ouest*
or quest or)

worry bead
relinquish

redolent as always
as the heated rose

summer and
a scent

(allot illusions as
is necessary to)

annealing praise
reticulate as tongue

mighty and a mouse
alike a maze

can he her up haul
or over if and may

asylum for her worship
in the night announce

the word of way
widen and weave

the was or is of
story is a story of

4.

* Order, gentlemen. Order

    ←———————————————————————————

is the ultimate
mountain. I raised my baton.

---

*I have removed from this stanza the single line

(her breasts were paradigms)

(originally in parenthesis, as indicated) because I am somewhat of-
fended by the offhand reference to paradigm. And yet, is not the
mother figure the figure at once most present in and most absent
from this poet's work? The concern with *nostos* is related to a long
family history of losses: *e.g.*, the paternal side of the family landing
in New York in June, 1841, aboard the *Pauline*, and the mother of
the large Kroetsch family, settled in Waterloo County, Ontario, a
few years thereafter widowed, the early death of the poet's mother
in Alberta, a century after that first un-homing. Both quest and
goal become paradigmatic (RK).

inhale, enact
the crappy sun

or face
finagle

far, and the body
wait

(the blackfoot had
no names for days)

the banjo, call
clairvoyant, still

gesticulate
triumphant

strum
and the morning

first, archaic
be, become

wrong or alone
we live, in delay's body

bone, altering
bone

after the word (after
which there can be no after)

cart
and the whipped horse

I lick your nipples
with my hand

5.

The bindertwine of place—
The mansource of the man—
The natural odour of stinkweed—
The ache at the root of
*
                              the spinal thrust—

←─────────────────────────────────────

(Despair is   not writing the poem
say what you will about despair.)

ROBERT KROETSCH

*Surely this is where the original version of the poem (1969) fails
(Ron Smith of Oolichan Books on Vancouver Island, pointing to
the reliance on dashes—the poet, come to a crucial moment in the
journey, hesitating to write the longish poem the occasion dictates.
The westward (and return) journey that fascinates Kroetsch is here
turned entirely into implication without adequate substance (i.e.,
ground), into, at best, intertext ... Only later do three couplets
suggest themselves, relating the journey to the poet's equal
fascination with the visit to the land of the dead (in search of?)—

(interior, the
dark shore)

the godfish
hole

the bait bait, and
the hung hook hang

—but it is too late now, too late to weld such post-surreal niceties
into a voice that in the sixties insisted on a source that was at once
oral and local (RK).

Weather Vane

muse
I figure

hold us, cock and after
after the hot sun

clydesdale or
and forecast if

under adam's gun
we live

or dithyramb
of sorts, allow

self, portraying
self

think you think
the globe round

the cupola
to deem or dream

trajectory
of ignorance

(the bent pine
resisting west)

wind, swing
the arrow's edge

6.

What I took to be an eagle
turned out to be a gull.
We glimpsed the sea.
The road ended

←—————————————————————————————

but it did not end:
the crying gulls turned
on the moon. The moon
was in the sea.
Despair that had sought the moon's
meaning found now the moon.
(Mile Zero is everywhere.)
The roar of the sea was the sea's roar.

128

ROBERT KROETSCH

1969/1981
Binghamton/Winnipeg

the story of the poem
become
the poem of the story
become

Collected Poem

Every year is the same:
it's different.

visions of
exactitude

Death is a live
issue.

The world is   always
ending.

When you get to the
beginning   stop.

Green apples make you
shit like a bird, or

once in a while, just over
the next low hill

legs are longer than arms with
few exceptions

why doesn't bogus
rhyme with slump

I want to see one square
cloud.

(tempus
forgets)

The tree is there every morning.
Maybe you noticed that too.

Time rewrites every book. We try so to construct a book
that time, rewriting, will make it better.

The world is ending, but
the world does not end.

ΓΡΑΜΜΑΤΑ ΣΤΗΝ ΘΕΣΣΑΛΟΝΙΚΗ

May 27.

Wednesday. I'm up at 4:00 A.M. I was up at 4:00, it's
5:00 now. Had tea. Prowled around our apartment. Our
home. Looked at Lacan. Looked at a poem I should work
on but won't let myself work on until this fall. But
should work on. Because your absence that fills this
apartment fills my mind at this hour. Thinking about
your mother, your father, your grandmother, all of you,
there in that Salonika apartment overlooking the
Acheiropoietos. The basilica housing (hiding?) the icon
that was not made by human hands. *Acheiropoietos.*

A typewriter full of words. I should buy a new one, a
typewriter packed with words, packed full. It is going to
be a hot day. The flow of days towards our meeting. The
novel teases me. The book almost exists. You hurt me into
this novel, by going away. Each dawn I make this discovery
of my love for you, a strange Columbus. Finding only that
my mouth hurts for you. My lips needing your hair, the skin
of your back. I bite your absence. I want the small scars
of your back, where you were cut, when a child, and sick;
cut with a razor and bled and healed. I want each scar to
be a little cunt that I can heat with my tongue.

May 28.

Sometimes I think this going away of yours has hurt me
beyond all repair. I am not myself and cannot ever be
again. I am my own emptiness, trying to fill my emptiness
with words. You were unkind. Unnatural. I search for a
way to hate myself free of your absence. But memory mocks
my pretending. I am a Columbus trying to sail away and
forget the finding. Columbus, who could not sail back to
Europe, because he had made his own Europe cease to exist.

I envy you your nightmares. A nightmare, one like yours,
would ground me in potential. But my actual dreams, my
dreams of each night, are empty. I have learned to dream
emptiness.

May 29.

Only one letter from you, in Greece. And you don't phone.
And I can't phone because you'll be out when I phone and I
can't handle the language problem with your parents.

I am tired of strawberries. One last basket to finish, and
then I must stop eating strawberries. I had some cherries
yesterday. They were outrageously expensive. Perhaps I
can measure my waiting in kinds of fruit. There, I am almost
through the strawberries, I have already begun the cherries.

I have neglected for a whole day to remember the clarity
of your collarbones.

Tournier, *The Ogre*. I have gone through a dozen novels,
looking for a clue, finding none, and now, in *The Ogre*,
I begin to get insights. Like Liebhaber, I begin to
remember forward.

May 30.

What am I supposed to do with the eggplant in the fridge?
It stares out at me when I open the fridge door. Perhaps
even it is lonesome. It is losing its lustre. It begins
to look small, forsaken, forlorn. I may snatch it out of
the fridge late one night, secretly destroy it. During the
day, for all its growing smallness, it remains powerful.
It reminds me of the colour of your eyes when you are angry.

I took my black oxfords, the shoes you don't like, to the
shoemaker behind the hotel on Pembina to have them resoled
and he said they aren't worth resoling. After I throw away
my black oxfords I'm going to throw away the eggplant. In
fact I may throw away black itself, defying that absence of
colour ever to colour my life again. I shall thereby refute
Greek widowhood. I think of your grandmother, serving
olives and bread and sliced tomatoes, pouring ouzo. I am,
today, my own widow.

May 31.

Tonight it's raining, a beautiful violent thunderstorm,
a prairie storm, coming straight at our kitchen window
from far in the south and I'm happy and desperate at the
same time, and I'm happy and I'm desperate at the same
time, and I'm happy. And I'm desperate. And C B C is on
strike and playing classical music. I sit here at the
kitchen window, between the storm and the radio.

I am past all fantasy, past even touching my own body.
Except only that I rehearse you with my remembering
tongue.

June 1.

(some days in summer
for a whole week
in Winnipeg
it's so warm
that women wear
short dresses and
men play tunes
fingering the
unseen stops with
all
ten fingers)

The trip begins to look definite. Gary Geddes phoned
tonight. I must have pictures taken for a visa. Seven of
us, writers, will leave on June 29, return July 10. Leave
through Vancouver, fly to Tokyo, then on to Peking. My
wanting to be in Salonika, my going to China.

Machines are puritans.
They do not know pleasure.

June 3.

Today is census day in Canada. I put you down as a
citizen living forever right here in Canada.

I'm outlining the Greek chapters of the novel. Sudden
and abrupt changes in the story, so I'm back to writing
first drafts. It's obvious that I'll be finishing the
book next summer, not this summer. And now I feel less
pressure to get the book finished.

Would you check something for me? Dorf gets a message from
the international police service. Interpol, I believe it's
called. Would the message be delivered by the local police
in Salonika? And—if that's the case—I'll need an exact
description of how the police look, dress ... I can't
remember ... Dorf, just a few minutes ago, was sitting
in a taverna in Salonika, lamenting that to love is a great
fault.

June 3, again.

This afternoon I went to the pool, and now my shoulders
feel pleasantly burned. I watched a woman, desirable in her
bikini, and I thought of you going to your island, going to
Sifnos, those hairs that are so indecent and exciting, those
hairs that your swimsuit can't contain and that you know are
exciting, and then your excitement, heightening the
excitement. I want to cup your cunt in my hand. I want
to suck your nipples. Here, tonight, in this heat. I want
the smell of you. Our bed has no smell, it has no secrets,
it has no life.

I've read more of Michaux, a fascinating travel journal,
Ecuador. A kind of mad poem. Or perhaps it really is a
travel journal. I don't know.

Part of living together is the allowing for repetition.
The nuance, the change, the exploration. The making strange.
The discovery within the known of what was known and
what was unknown and what is mystery. My needing you
tonight, not a mere stranger in a bikini. My needing the
larger and genuine mystery of us, not the complete known
of a stranger.

June 4.

No mail at all from you. None. I talk to myself. I
begin to suspect I am writing these letters to myself,
writing myself the poem of you. Its title is, *I Think
About Women Much of the Time*. That is the poem about
you and your silence.

Tonight I read Milosz, his selected poems, a book I found
in Mary Scorer Books, and I stopped sometimes in the
presence of his lines. His lines are pure lines, even in
translation, that strike little gaps into the world:

"What constitutes the training of the hand?"

(The novel is going badly.) (I went downtown in the rain
to look for books on China and didn't find any.) (Yes, I
am to leave here on the 29th of June.) (I find it hard to
imagine the apartment vacant, the lights not coming on at
night, the red teakettle never set on a burner, the bedroom
always empty of sound.)

June 5.

The basilica. There in Salonika. The icon, not made by
human hands. You, with your parents, with your grand-
mother, on the balcony overlooking the Acheiropoietos.
The grounds, around the church, where, as a child, you
played. Where the two boy-children touched your cunt.
Acheiropoietos. Now, you, eating melon from the gardens
of Salonika.

Ken Probert and I went for a beer. It is, after all, Friday
night. I am home and I miss you and I ask, as we asked in
the campus pub, what, then, is love? And of course I know
the answer. But you are not here. So I must find an answer
in the absence of the answer. I am baking two potatoes. One
for you and one for me. That is not love. The steak is in
the fridge. I am sick and tired of steak. But all I know about
cooking is how to bake a potato and how to broil a steak.
One potato, two potatoes, three potatoes, four. It was a
childhood game. I do not remember the game, but I
remember the words.

ROBERT KROETSCH

June 7.

Yes, I helped Cooley tear down the roof that had been built
over the back porch of his cottage. It was mostly done when
I got there. Then we had a beer and a huge steak supper,
a delicious meal, my sitting at the table with Dennis and
Diane while the kids were called and didn't show up; then
all of us having dessert together. Then, in front of the
fire in the living room, our talking about Dorothy Livesay,
from whom the Cooleys bought the cottage. Where Dorothy
talked, held court. The continuities of change.

Late, late at night, driving south from Lake Winnipeg,
driving alone, into the city.

> A dark as dark as a dark.
> A moon as moon as a moon.
> My lust doth rage in this
> of mine old body.

June 8.

The logic of your beauty runs away from my eyes.

From you I could learn to hate geography. Its emptiness.
Its spaces.

Penelope was the artist, in that story. Odysseus, only
the dumb and silent one, approaching and being unravelled
and approaching again. Odysseus, unravelled, approaching.
Penelope gave the story to herself. She did not give the
story to Odysseus.

Ken Probert and I went for a late lunch, this afternoon,
to the new Burger King that has just opened on Pembina.
Grand Opening. Little children, wearing crowns. The
children, in their make-believe, laughing. I asked for
a crown. The young gentleman in charge of the crowns
was offended.

June 9.

It's the middle of the night and I can't sleep. I had a
snack—peaches and cream, yummy. No bread in the house
for breakfast. The fridge is empty. In Greece it's
daytime and you're wide awake, it doesn't seem right. I
want to snuggle up with you in the same time zone.

Our second date lasted for four years. I remember our
beginning it with Wellek's boring lecture and our impatience
to be together and to go for a drink. And the whole week-
end with no one being able to find you, and your Greek
friend meeting us, by accident, in the shopping centre north
of Binghamton, and spilling the beans: may her pussy turn
into a mousetrap! And I remember our nights in the
Fischlers' house, while they were in France on sabbatical
leave, and the ghost that would walk up the creaking stairs,
late at night, while you were downstairs reading, and I was
upstairs reading. And we were polite and waited until it
went up to the attic. And then we would wait again, to
see who would dare to climb the stairs, who to descend.

June 15.

I'm back from the Collingwood Poetry Weekend. Five FIVE *five* letters from you today. I kissed the photograph, *icon*ographic. And never touched.

In Collingwood, I went to Steve McCaffery's seminar, and he is a gentle and brilliant man. And Chris Dewdney is far into the testing of a new dream vision, located in the mind where the mind literally dreams. And Andy Suknaski and I entered into his Romanian sorrow together and went outside into the sun and played catch with the two gloves and the softball that he'd remembered to bring along. And Eli Mandel has whole new theories of the poem to let bloom at the rain forest edge of (THE COAST IS ONLY A LINE) this westering of ours.

And Gary Geddes was there, with the details of the trip to China. I do not have enough stories of China to be able to imagine the China that I should be imagining. Marco Polo, forgive us all.

June 16.

What is a letter? Sometimes it is a star that fell.
Sometimes it is a rock, a stone.

June 16, again.

Your language has changed, in Greece. When you left,
English was your first language. Now it is your second
again. I hear the transformation in your letters.

Yours is a complex ritual of place and culture. I come
from huge silences. Strange, that I so long ago borrowed
the sound of Greece. I always heard the biblical stories
as something a little bit bizarre, grotesque. Even that
version of the garden story, for all my obsession with stories
of the garden. But the Greek stories, for all their passion
and violence, spoke *exactly* to me. I could find no
mismatching between me and them. Except for the distance.
The actual place of those stories was distant. Except that
you erased that distance. I have, in my images of childhood,
so many images of distance … But that's another story.

In Greece I found a maze and stories of mazes that became,
I now see, metonymous with my own life.

Suknaski and I, pretending to be god's fools, and then,
to our horror, finding out that we really are. And then,
at the possible centre of the possible maze, the possible
trickster god.

June 17.

Form. I want to talk to you about the relationship of the
erotic to form. But I fall silent. I receive a letter from
you and it's so old that you are already someone else, the
letter is out of joint with the reality that I imagine. A
problem in form, a dislocation that is real.

I dream, and the tooth
broken

first, archaic
be

undone.

June 18.

4:30 A.M.

I want to read your nipples with my tongue.

That sentence, in my mind. As I awoke.

The rain, the rain, the lovely rain talks to my windows.
You are the poem of my hurt.

      talking the
      world

      the mind, unshelve
      itself, in this
      the
      earthquake time

      wind your clock
      with a rope,
      never bite a hollow
      radish

June 19.

Lying on your side of the bed this morning. I looked at
the frame of the mirror on your dresser. Making strange.
The shaved wood. Needing oil now. The curved lines, in
the wood around the glass. The mirror holding in its stare
the room. Yesterday, phoning you, expecting you to be
in Salonika, back from Athens. You on your quest, me
here at home. I've burned up half our woodpile. Loneliness
and a fire. Loneliness is a fire. Sending a book to your
mother today, a copy of *The Criminal Intensities of Love as
Paradise*, a book of which she will not be able to read a
word. Language, too, gone back to its corner. Cathay.
Li Po and Tu Fu, those contrary poets. I read them. Then
I read Seferis again, Ritsos again. My tonight, tonight,
is already your tomorrow. We have unhinged the calendar,
cracked the globe:

the despair of the poet on meeting
reality.

June 21.

the city-woman
the city/woman

I should be able to work from today until the 29th, when I supposedly go to China. Though I can hardly believe that prophecy. And if I can't work I'll throw the tent into the old Dodge Dart and go to a park or a forest somewhere... I begin to sound like The Sad Phoenician of Love ... "but I'm all right now, don't feel you should worry!"

But I'm supposed to go to Calgary in two days. To do the sound track for John Snow's film. His sculptures of women. With me reading passages from my work. I think about women. My voice is scratchy. Get a steamer, the doctor tells me. That's what my Aunt Annie told me, years ago. That's how I got the scar on my chest, trying to steam myself and scalding myself in the bargain. Those days we used a pan of hot water and camphor and a towel. I was home alone that day too.

June 22.

to desire an end to desire
is to desire

and, sometimes, looking at your ass, your legs, I see the
old Greek woman you are going to be one day, you with
your city woman's view of the peasants, and I love you then,
I want to be old with you, both of us hundreds of years
old, and still loving each other, making tea and getting
drunk and kissing in public and still writing ferocious
poems to each other

(We are scheduled to have dinner on July 26 on Galiano
Island in the Pink Geranium Restaurant with Audrey
Thomas and Pauline Butling and Fred Wah.)

And I'm delighted that you're going back to your magical
isle, to Sifnos, again; to the July heat and the lovely,
crowded buses and the cliff-edge trails that are called
roads. I am so much the farmer that I cannot forget those
stone walls, those terrace walls, built by hands and backs
and lives. Those tiny, flat fields, rimmed in stone. The
fig trees.

June 24.

Just back from Calgary and exhausted, but I slept for an
hour on the plane and feel perversely awake now; a midnight
flight, up so high in the darkness I could see a glow of
light on the northern horizon; these longest days; and I
remember as a child, in June, seeing that same light from
the north windows of our Alberta house, the sun set but
casting a visible arctic light. It was a secret thrill.
This high counterpoint to your Greek seas.

     ((O Lowry, how you must have rejoiced when you
        realized the others could only succeed, while

       you could fail.

     ((I have aspired to all forms of folly; now
       I am being wise.

     ((the pleasure, this cool June night,
       in putting on
       a sweater

June 24, later.

You call me, wake me out of a deep sleep, to wish me happy
birthday—on the WRONG day: you can remember the
name day of about forty-five people including every lover
you've been to bed with more than twice sometimes I think
you should get a bulk rate on your mail to Greece but when
it comes to my birthday, NO, you can't get it, I'm Ramonde
Atteste Fidelus, born June 31, just after the first green
moon of the century, we've actually lived together, I'm
the son of an itinerant Japanese rodeo rider and a saskatoon
bush that was in full flower, even last year, when you went
out on my birthday and bought YOURSELF a beautiful
gift I attributed it all to mere revenge and a high Greek
sense of tragic irony, but when you call me because you're
going to your astrologer and you don't know if the
conjunction...

There's the threat of a mail strike here in Canada. Find us a
house to rent on Sifnos. This is too much.

June 25.

I walk such edges of the trembling soul that the nightbirds
cannot sleep. More rain in Vancouver than ever recorded in
history. Love is an absence of middles.

                                        the old
                                        poet, in his cups
                                        and thinking   as
                                        usual   of

all this, and
your body, now
tonight

in my hands/mouth
tasting the sting
of you, the burn

of your desire
an acid, etching
the mind blank

drain my eyes
to the darkness of
your pubic hair

the lick, a
stabbing
of my tongue, hungry

I want
no words, tonight
dream your lovers

but the mind, broken
of words
into desire

my breaking cry that
will not break
and still, then

no words, no
names for
the world is/was

June 26.

THE POET, ALONE, ON HIS 54TH BIRTHDAY,
REFLECTS ON HIS 54TH BIRTHDAY.

June 27.

A dream of living. No ... We must live our living.

When you get to Sifnos, take another look at the house
you mentioned. The one by the chapel. The one that you
said we might be able to rent a year from now. I
was standing there on that hilltop, beside the chapel,
looking down over the village to the sea, when an old
woman came from that house; she walked out behind
that whitewashed house and flung a potful of piss onto the
garden. It fell as a golden rain, the flung piss, onto the
dew-wet green of the garden.

I think of the Chinese poems I'm reading these days, so
many of them about travel and separation.

June 28.

By meaning we mean something that means
but, in the process, means its opposite.

We write books to avoid
writing books.

from you, from Pound, from the Chinese:

Σέ παραχαλῶ πές μου ἀπό πρίν ὅτι
θἄρθεις,
Καί θἄρθω νά σέ συναντήσω
        πέρα στήν Τσό-Φού-Σά.

Postcards from China

To my daughters,
Margaret and Laura:

July 1

Flying over the Chinese coast, off the China Sea and
towards Shanghai; in the green land far below us, what I
took to be roads. There cannot be so many roads in China,
I thought, roads everywhere. And then, a few minutes later,
I realized that what I took to be roads were canals, ditches,
waterways. It was a web of water below us, the Chinese land.

I thought again of a man I met in the Vancouver Airport,
while waiting for the flight to Tokyo. We were standing in
a check-in line together, this man and I, and when he asked
me where I was going and why I explained that I was going
to China as a writer. And that man, then, was silent for a
while; and then he said: I am a man with no language. And
he explained: he was the son of a Japanese soldier stationed
in Korea during the Second World War. His mother was
Korean. He had not quite learned Japanese. He had not
quite learned Korean. He had come to Canada and had not
quite learned either English or French.

I am in China without a language. What I saw from the sky
was roads that weren't roads; I saw the irrigation system
for watering the land and from up in the sky I thought I
saw roads, too many of them, brown, on the green of the
green earth, and then I saw all those roads were water, and
so in a sense they were roads, and I thought of the fingering

water, holding the land green; it was like that, I was happy to see that, and I understood; but then we were landing.

That was the Shanghai Airport. Now, a few hours later, in Peking, I think of you, my daughters, there on the other side of the world, as innocent of China today as I was yesterday. We come unaware to these tidal changes in our lives.

July 2

You must have a guide when you go on a journey to a mysterious, unknown place; that's one of the rules of literature, and maybe of life also. As it happens, we have three guides, and that makes it even better.

Mr. Bi is one of our guides. Mr. Bi Shou-wang is a stoutish, older man with a face that has seen too much, and therefore he smiles with his eyes instead of with his mouth. He is a poet who knows hundreds of poems in Chinese that he cannot tell us, but he has learned to sing songs in English, and when we are driving around, all of us in a wonderful little bus, seven Canadian writers and our guides and our driver, and when we begin to sing because we are happy, Mr. Bi begins to sing, out of his sad face, songs like "Red River Valley." I suspect he is a direct descendant of a Tang warlord.

Mr. Wong is our translator. He has the tough, wiry body of a rodeo rider, and the tough wiry mind of a poet who is too wise to write poems. He translates with ease and humour and generosity, as if everything said must be wise and good.

All the women in our group, Susan Paradis and Alice Munro and Adele Wiseman, are, I can tell, in love with Mr. Wong, who is in love with words and the way they try to buck him off. I know that you would love him too, if you were here.

Our third guide is Madame Fan. Like Mr. Bi she is a poet, and like Mr. Wong she is a translator. She worries about us Canadians. I can see that her assignment is to worry about us. She worries that we aren't eating enough, though we are stuffed with huge meals three times a day, and she worries at the amount of beer we Canadians drink, and she worries that the ferocious sun of this long drought will strike us all down in our tracks and she took us to a small, delightful store and allowed us to buy straw hats. My straw hat is too small. Madame Fan doesn't seem to worry about that, however.

The Forbidden City is a place of magic roofs. The tile roofs are golden and dare to imitate the sun. Only dragons dare to land on the roofs. There are nine thousand rooms in this palace. I have been into ten of them.

Tonight we had dinner with a group of Chinese writers. We had duck for dinner. The whole meal was duck. I've come to like using chopsticks. One member of our party is in danger of starving because she can't use chopsticks. But I like them. Throw away your knives and forks. Eat duck. We started with feet of duck. The gizzard, to me, is not quite so good as chicken gizzard. But the heart is a delicacy. And the head, split open after being roasted, is full of surprises for the palate. Wash all this down with tall brown bottles of Chinese beer. And two kinds of duck soup. Yes, the soup came at the end of the meal. And each and every dish is placed on a lazy Susan, in the middle of the round table, and passes before you. And you have to be quick with your chopsticks. Especially to eat soup.

The bicycle riders are dancing. It is a dance of silence
in the long, wide, straight streets of Peking. The wheat
is spread today, on the pavement, to dry. The dancers are
offering praise.

Today we went to many places, and one of them was the New
Summer Palace. Yiheyuan. Garden of Harmony in Old Age.
I went there hoping to catch a glimpse of Buddha, so I
climbed the Hill of Longevity, and damned near died doing
it; we all of us climbed up hundreds of stone steps. I
saw a lotus, in flower, in a small pond, high up the
stairway. A lotus in flower is as beautiful as Peking
seen from the Cloud-Dispelling Hall. From half-way up the
hill we could see, through a mist of fine rain, down to
Kumming Lake and its little boats, down to the golden
glazed-tile roofs of Peking, the roofs that are like
tent-tops turned ornate and golden, and so beautiful that
I knew, secretly, that if I tried I could fly like a dragon
and land on a roof. We climbed all the way up the steep
stairway to the Pavilion of the Fragrance of Buddha. And
we went inside, into the tall, high gloom, into a room that
was big enough for Buddha himself. But Buddha wasn't
there. But I wasn't surprised, I knew I had climbed the hill
to find, to admire, to love a lotus blossom.

We had lunch in the Hall for Listening to Orioles Singing. I
was happy, thinking about Buddha, who had stepped out of
his Pavilion, somehow, before I got there. I thought about
the lotus in blossom and the golden glazed-tile roofs, the
tiles like the scales on the most beautiful fish in the world;
and we ate fish, and we drank more good Chinese beer.
Or maybe I have this wrong. Maybe we ate the lunch and
then went and climbed the Hill of Longevity and looked for
Buddha. In any case, there was a fine rain falling, more of a
mist than a rain, and we could and we couldn't see what we
were seeing. And I think it was yesterday we went to the
Forbidden City. China is a garden and a maze. We went

tonight to the Peking Opera, here, in Peking. And a male actor, a man in his forties, acting in "The Drunken Beauty," in a matter of minutes persuaded me that he was a young woman, and beautiful, and sad, and disappointed in love, and getting drunk. And I am in China.

Imagine my surprise when I sat down beside Joseph Conrad at a crowded table in the rooftop restaurant of the Friendship Hotel. It was a hot night. "It's none of my business, Mr. Conrad," I said, "but frankly, a lot of people would be surprised to see you here in China." He looked surprised, under his ridiculous white jungle hat. "How so?" he said. "Well," I said. I was being discreet. "You were born in 1857." "Quite so, quite so," he said, trying to sound British.

But I could see he had forgotten the year of his birth. He's showing his age. And then he added, suddenly, powerfully, "I've never been here myself." And the voice, Laura; you should have heard him. But I was puzzled by his statement. "I've never been here myself." And there he was, right beside me. I noticed his beer bottle was empty. I jumped up and went into the small room where two young women were sweating in the dim light, one of them snapping the tops off bottles, the other making change for the *yuan* notes, using an abacus. When I got back to the table with the beer, Mr. Conrad was nowhere to be seen. I looked silly, a full bottle in my hand, another at my place. "Thirsty tonight?" someone said. And before I could answer or ask, "It's the drought does it," he said. The stranger. "The worst in two hundred years."

July 4

Tea, in the cool dawn, while I sit at the old and ornate desk, here in my room, and look out under the bamboo strips that shade my window. Hot water from the huge thermos. The tea steeping in a lidded cup.

There are dragons everywhere. Dragons carved in stone. Painted dragons. Dragons made of tile, of jade. I have asked my guides what dragons stand for and each guide gives me a different explanation. Finally, I begin to understand.

I have come to China to read the future. A Chinese poet can look back to the *Shih-Ching*, a collection of poems put together about 600 B.C. Before Plato and Socrates had their confabs.

Today we had lunch in the Canadian Embassy. How quickly knives and forks have come to seem affected, strange, not immediate and direct. Chopsticks, Meggie, become the hand, the fingers. They are becoming.

Today we had tea with Madame Ding Ling. She works in this newfangled form, the novel. Twenty-one years, she spent, "in the country." For having the courage to speak her truth, a Chinese woman's truth. To go to her apartment is to sit, humbly, in the presence of courage. She has a beautiful granddaughter who reminded me of you; the granddaughter is studying English ... There are dragons, everywhere.

July 5

The Great Wall looks as if it must have kept China in, not the barbarians out. It is a frame on China, a long frame, unimaginably crooked, hung on top of mountain ridges. I walked my feet to blisters, following my eyes.

Two boys selling green apricots, where the buses park, and we were hungry for fresh fruit and bought apricots from a hand-held scale and Gary Geddes and Patrick Lane and Geoff Hancock managed to eat at least enough, perhaps too many.

We had a picnic at the site of the Ming Tombs. A picnic here is not out on the grass, it's out of a basket. We sat around tables in a gracious building that seems to have been prepared, complete with private rooms and waiters, especially for picnics. But the picnic lunch was huge: we ate boiled eggs and great thick slices of bread, and we ate chicken, and we drank the orange drink that seems to be everywhere in China, a version of Orange Crush.

The Great Wall. The Ming Tombs. They are forms of creation that exist independent of literature. So much death in the wall, in the tombs. They are only a few kilometres apart. The wall and the tombs. And everywhere the hard fact of the peasants' lives. People stooped in the rice paddies. Two fishermen on a raft, fishing with cormorants. Four women digging a ditch. The commune houses, low, blending into the earth. The flocks of ducks beside the ponds. The three-horse teams, hauling loads of pipe, of steel rods, into the city. The bicycles, loaded with hay, with crates, with families. The tall willow trees along the road. The fields of eggplant and corn and beans. Wheat spread to dry on a paved highway. The groups of workers, perhaps twenty-five in a group, men and women, young and old, putting fertilizer on the land by hand, the bags of fertilizer spaced about the fields, the workers going with pans to get more fertilizer, then spreading it by hand. In China: hands and hoes and shovels. Feet, in the dust, in the mud.

Peking: the city itself, being rebuilt, and mostly by hand. We took a cab downtown, tonight, and made a mistake in giving directions. We are let off in an area where workers live; we came upon a boy, seated in the narrow street, strumming a guitar. Gary accepted the guitar from the boy and began to play and in a matter of moments we had an audience of two hundred faces, there in the dimly lit street. We sang the surprise of ourselves, we writers, to the astonished audience. To our own ears, Country & Western.

July 6

The National Museum. My ecstasy at seeing the Tang horses. I experienced ecstasy, Meggie. Whatever that is. The Tang Dynasty, 618–907. The horses are singing. What you used to say, Laura, when we rode the carousel, there in the park in Binghamton, New York. Those perfect horses gave me transport. I was, for almost a minute, resident and present and alive in the Tang Dynasty.

Today we flew to Xi'an. Xi'an was the capital during the Tang Dynasty. The four-propeller plane. Our keeping cool by fanning ourselves, the folding fans distributed by the stewardess, who is plainly dressed in the Chinese costume, pale shirt and darker slacks and sandals. Blue or green, mostly. The temperature when we landed: 38 degrees Celsius.

Unexpectedly, I saw Buddha. But there were three of him, three statues, surrounded by eighteen disciples, in a hall I entered when I was looking for the place where the great poet, Tu Fu, got drunk and wrote poems. Tu Fu, the Tang poet, was up on top of the Greater Wild Goose Pagoda, having a sip of wine with Joseph Conrad. I could hear them but I couldn't see them. The pagoda was built in 652 to house the Buddha sutras; Xuan Zhuang walked to India to get them, and then walked back, with 657 sutras, and made the whole trip in a mere 17 years. The pagoda, seven stories high, was built to house the sutras. In the garden around the pagoda I met a young man who has studied English for a few years but had never spoken to a person who speaks English and he spoke to me, he said, "I am studying photography," and when I answered him he was astonished, he couldn't believe that I really understood him, I responded to his comments, but every so often he would ask, "Do you really understand me?" as if I were only being polite, or pretending, and then he realized he was really speaking the language he had studied, and we embraced and had ourselves photographed, because he was studying photography.

Here, where the Silk Route began. This morning I got up
early and had my tea, and then I went for a walk in the
bright morning light to watch people doing their exercises,
in the parks. And I saw an old man, walking. In a garden.
In a garden that to me seemed to be a maze, a pattern of
hedges and paths; one of those gardens designed especially
to tease us out of our habitual ways. Like the Forbidden
City, in Peking, that unfolds and contradicts and confuses
with impossible repetitions. He was following paths, the
old man, making turns, pleasing himself with surprise and
mystery. Himself stopping, now and then; he watched
those about him, doing tai chi, while I watched him
watching. One could lose the world, here in Xi'an. There is
no music, not a book or magazine, not a neon sign or sound
of traffic that is familiar. I was lost and trying to find
a post office. I wanted to mail you a card I had written.
In a Chinese post office there's a little brush and a glue pot,
so you can seal your letter.

We visited the Forest of Steles. Housed in what were once
Confucian temple buildings. Slabs of stone with, carved
on them, pictures and poems. Calligraphy, that art where
hand and mind become synonymous. Two young men were
making a print, patting a stone with a cloth dipped in ink.
The sound of their patting like a muffled drum.

The underground army. Buried in loess by the endless wind
from Mongolia. Buried by the emperor, Qin Shi Huang, who
united China and built the Great Wall, who buried himself
here in this tomb, in 211 B.C. He surrounded his tombs with
armies of life-sized figures, in *terra cotta*, armed with real
weapons. Six thousand figures, horses and men. Peasants,
in 1974, digging a well to fight a drought, found ghostly
figures in the earth. The archaeology of dream. And now,
I cannot forget, the handsome men, the proud horses,
rising into this scalding heat from the Chinese earth. This
breaking into light.

Up early to fly to Canton. Guangzhou. Fanning ourselves:
perhaps the fans fanning are what makes us fly. And then
we could not get into the airport in Guangzhou, because of
a typhoon. We turned and went west, inland again; we found
ourselves flying over the karst country of subtropical
China; thrust up from the green fields, the towering
pinnacles of limestone. It is hardly a mortal landscape, it
seems, rather, left over from a dream. The soldiers of that
first emperor, back there in Xi'an, turned into stone.
Forever and never, breaking into light.

My last bed, here in China. Over my bed is a huge mosquito
net. It hangs from the high ceiling like a cornucopia and
covers the whole bed. A banquet, tonight in Guangzhou.
With Madame Fan and Mr. Wong. With the gracious poets
who host us in this city. Mr. Wong translates our
conversation, translates our poems. I read from "Seed
Catalogue," here at this feast from a garden world. Lotus
seeds. Quails' eggs. Frogs' legs. We drink toasts.
Cinnamon wine. A stern-looking waiter fills our delicate
glasses, fills them again and again, and again we drink
toasts. Seven appetizers and ten main dishes and four
desserts. The cat is delicious, Meggie. I am less fond of
snake. I don't much like the texture. One could justify
a flight to China, simply to eat fresh lichee nuts.

Taking the train, from Guangzhou to Hong Kong. After the
typhoon. I sit here, sipping tea from my lidded cup. I
watch through the large windows of this modern train. I
watch through the windows. The thousands and more
thousands of people, out in the ruined fields. The peasants,
picking up, after the typhoon. Perhaps a typhoon is a
dragon. And now the sky was so clear, so calm. The water
buffaloes, moving with slow patience, in the rice paddies.
The thousands of people, in the fields, in the ditches, on

the roads. With shovels and hoes. Threshing rice with little hand-run machines. Men and animals, wading in the water. Men and women and children, together, salvaging the stooked sheaves of rice. Each small sheaf like a paintbrush, raised to the making of this landscape of hope.

: the calendar of *anthropos*
  is the clown-god's whip*

It seems that from the beginning the sanctuary of Delphi has been the object of innumerable plots.

— Pausanias, 2nd Century A.D.

What can we say for certain? The day was sure to be a clear one; Meg reported that at breakfast. She had, while her sister was in the shower, taken a picture of the Parthenon. The Hotel Herodion is under the Acropolis. My room faced on the walled garden where late-night drinkers whispered in various tongues to the grape vines and the waiters. Meg took a picture. The window framed the picture she would take: high on the sunlit rock, the Parthenon in profile to the August-morning light. I was drinking too much coffee while my daughters, Laura and Meg, ate honeydew melon and sampled the feta. We had not finished our eating when the driver came into the breakfast room, his eyes naming us.

---

* fragment from "The Eggplant Poems"

: the glyph on the broken stone
  raises the eye, reads the tongue

We were, it turned out, taking a bus to catch our bus.
We were the only passengers, my two American daughters
and I, until the driver stopped at
another hotel and a Japanese lady
came up the stairwell of the bus,
an elegant lady so small our greetings
went over her head. She was wearing a
soft white hat with two plastic buttons
pinned discreetly on the left side, one
of them reading, OUZO POWER. She had
brought along her smile. She put it
on. The streets of Athens were morning
streets; I wanted coffee at a sidewalk
cafe. But the driver thumbed his horn
at all of Constitution Square. We
turned into a side street. We were
unloaded from the bus, for sorting
according to language:

Greek
English
German
French
Italian

Pausanias's Description of Greece,
translated with a commentary by J. G.
Frazer (Macmillan and Co., Limited,
St. Martin's Street, London, 1913):
*All the twenty-seven names of the Olympic
trophy occur on the Delphic trophy, but
the order is somewhat different, and on
the Delphic trophy there are four names
… which, if Pausanias's list is
correct, did not appear on the Olympic
trophy. How are these discrepancies
to be explained?*

Lacedaemonians
Athenians
Corinthians
Tegeans
Sicyonians
Aeginetans
Megarians
Epidaurians
Orchomenians
Phliasians
Troezenians
Hermionians
Tirynthians
Plataeans
Thespians
Mycenaeans
Ceans
Melians
Tenians
Naxians
Eretrians
Chalcidians
Canadians
Styrians
Eleans
Potidaeans
Leucadians
Anactorians
Cythnians
Siphnians
Ambraciots
Lepreans

171

Completed Field Notes

: the chariot fell
  into the sky

and, going to Delphi, going to Delphi, I had expected
to ask a question, the three of us on the bus, the morning
ride, into morning, my daughters with me, there on the road
to Delphi

going to Delphi, a father, his two daughters

                              Laura, entering college in
                              the fall: We could ask if
                              acid rain will dissolve the
                              world, make it as pure as
                              glass, as empty.

going to Delphi,
a question, seeking
a speaker

into a forest
of olive trees

going to Delphi

                              and Margaret, to her father:
                              Why do you want to be a tree?

I want to be an *olive* tree, I explained, not just any old
tree; one of those ancient olive trees, with holes clean
through the trunk, where you can see out the other side.
To what? Meg said. To other olive trees, I explained

going to Delphi

:   the [Pythian] silence

and the voice on the loudspeaker system:
                                    Marathon. That
place over there [that we've just passed, that you almost
saw] is Marathon. The messenger, when the Persians were
defeated, ran all the way to Athens. They had no Key Tour
buses then [laughter]. He ran those twenty-two miles [the
precious words, locked on his tongue]. His message spoken
[the victory spoken, the city saved] he fell down dead.

and the voice on the loudspeaker system:
                                    Thebes. That
small town that you see just over there was once [famous,
I did not dare add, for its fresh water, for its abundance
of trees] a city. It was levelled stone by stone by the
Macedonians [of Alexander the Great].

and if   and when I fell asleep,
                                lulled by the bus, and my
                                head tilted and teetered,
                                almost fell off, Meg woke
                                me up with her

                                [daughterly]

                                giggling

and if
the [abandoned]
poem
speaks

We stopped for coffee. The bus stopped. We filed out,
all of us, out of the bus, through categories of trade,
T-shirts, postcards, cups and saucers with pictures on
them of Mt. Parnassus.

I sat down, over coffee, under the big windows, by a woman
from Australia. She was in her late seventies, travelling
alone, alone for six weeks, in Europe. She praised the
beauty of my daughters. Her eyebrows were soft white
caterpillars that moved on her forehead when she spoke.
We talked of weather, of crops, the woman from Australia
and I. Her husband, long dead, had been a wheat farmer.
During the war, she explained, he had trained in Canada.
Aircrew. He had seen the wheatfields of Canada. He was
killed in a crash. That was her first husband. Her second
husband, he too was dead.

174

ROBERT KROETSCH

Pausanias, the ordinary
traveller, of whom Sir
James Frazer said: *Without
him the ruins of Greece
would for the most part be
a labyrinth without a clue,
a riddle without an
answer.*

What did he eat, along the
way? What drinks did he
stop for? Did he meet old
ladies who spoke to strangers
of husbands dead in the wars?
What was the road like,
without buses? Were the
washrooms clean? Did fathers
travel with their daughters,
and weep in the night for
love?

Pausanias, the ordinary
traveller:

(Bk. VII ACHAIA, Ch. XXIII, Pt. 1) *I have also heard say
that the water of the Selemnus is a cure for love in man
and woman, for they wash in the river and forget their
love. If there is any truth in this story, great riches
are less precious to mankind than the water of the Selemnus.*

: the holes in the cheese contain the cheese

And behind us, on the seats behind us, talking across the
aisle as we talked across the aisle, three women from New
Jersey: three braggart women, baggy-faced, rich-bitch
clothing and one of the three painted to look like a child,

Sir James Frazer: ... *the*
Delphians decreed that for
the future the oracles
should be pronounced, not
by a virgin, but by a woman
over fifty years of age,
attired as a virgin.

all of them jangling their gold
in our ears, and asking each
other: How will we get our
stuff through Customs? They
schemed and plotted, one
deciding which three blouses
to wear through Customs,
another planning to fill her
brassiere (How will we get

our stuff through Customs?) with Turkish coins. They heard
from a conversation behind us that the site of Delphi is all
up and down, not level. We should have stayed in Athens
and gone shopping, they told each other. And my young
daughters looked daggers across the aisle to me, intending
their glances to swerve, become eagles, become thunder-
bolts ...

Sir James Frazer, in
response to Pausanias's
doubt (he believed in the
gods, in the heroes) as to
whether the Celts possessed
an art of divination
(x, xxi, 2):

The Celts practised divination
by means of human sacrifices;
the victim was stabbed in the
back and omens were drawn
from his convulsions ...
Justin mentions that, before
engaging in battle with Anti-
gonous, king of Macedonia,
the Gauls slew victims and
drew omens from their entrails.

:   eat your breakfast before lunch;
    buy shoes for both feet

on the dangerous road to Delphi, Oedipus, King of Thebes:

The Cleft Way

*From this point the high
road to Delphi grows
steeper and more difficult
to a man on foot. Many and
diverse are the tales told
about Delphi, and still
more about the oracle of
Apollo.* (Pausanias. His
scattered Greece under
Roman rule.)

It is always that way, the poem, the abandoned poem, in
which the hero, seeking the answer to the impossible
question, seeking the impossible question, takes to the road.
Hero. Eros. The evasion that is the meeting. The impossible
road.

It is always that way.
Swing with the road's high
curve, upward, past the
bauxite mines (spilling the
mountain ochre and orange).
And the first glimpse, over
the fell and crisscross
hills, a gap, agape; and a
shaped stone (broken); and
on its slant of (shaping)
stone, under the sky-high
cliff:

The city of Delphi stands wholly on a slope, and not only
the city, but also the sacred close of Apollo. The close is
very spacious, and is situated at the highest part of the city
... I will mention what seemed to me the most noteworthy
of the votive offerings.

We blundered our way out of the bus,
into a line where we might buy tickets,
at seventy drachmas each, a ticket
blank on one side, on the other an
almost pale green, to the left in grey
and white a drawing of the head of
Socrates, balding, bearded; to the
right of the drawing, first in Greek,
then in English: YOU HAVE KILLED,
O DANAOI, THE MOST LEARNED
WHO EVER CAUSED GRIEF: THE
NIGHTINGALE OF THE MUSES,
THE VERY BEST OF THE GREEKS

The Sacred Way. We began
our ascent of the Sacred Way,
a letter "s" in reverse, ascending
the slope. We prepared to ascend
(we entered in); we found our
guide. *On entering the precinct*
you see [you do not see] *a bronze*
bull made by Theopropus, an
Aeginetan, and dedicated by the
Corcyraeans. It is said that in
Corcyra a bull used to leave the
herd and the pasture to go down and bellow by the sea-
shore. The same thing happened every day, till the herdsman
went down to the shore and beheld a countless shoal of
tunnies. He told the Corcyraeans in the city, and they, after
labouring in vain to catch them, sent envoys to Delphi, and
in consequence they sacrificed the bull to Poseidon, and
immediately after the sacrifice they caught the fish; and
with the tithe of their take they dedicated the offerings at
Olympia and Delphi.

:   the gnomon is all
    that remains

We were under a cliff. On the Sacred Way. The sloping
pathway, under a cliff. Meggie would take no pictures.
She wanted, first, her own silence, against the silence
of the cliff, as if even the sound of her camera might
snap that spur of Mt.
Parnassus down upon us,
that story, of Earth,
of Gaia, and her sacred
spring, and its guardian
serpent, and Apollo, the
new god, killing the   persons
serpent, killing his way   guilty of
into mercy, there, under   sacrilege
his temple   were

(we were climbing toward   flung
his temple; we stopped to
stare at the Treasury of   down the
the Athenians; we stopped   (above)
to catch our breath)
                                         cliff

the dark and underworld
force of the earth,   (Jack and
struck into a speaking   Jill went
splendour, into a prophetic,   (quite a tumble
a singing, splendour

                                         into the
                                         Arkoudorema
                                         (the Bear's
                                         Gully

                                         (belly)

After the hard questions we ask the question, What? What
did you say? And the wind blowing. And how the wind
came up, and the dust, I don't know. The wind was blowing.
The feet of the tourists powdered the dust. What was it I
said I said? I said to Laura.

the   Pausanias: *What the Delphians*
                                       call the Navel (omphalos) *is*
belly   *made of white marble, and is*
                                       said by them to be at the centre
button   *of the whole earth, and Pindar*
                                       in one of his odes agrees with
of the world   *them.*

where two eagles

flying from the world's ends

met

(meet?)

Meggie was taking pictures. Laura and I stood behind the
omphalos and Meggie took a picture. Meggie and Laura
stood behind the omphalos and I took a picture. Meggie and
I stood behind the omphalos and Laura took a picture.

How does one pose for a   Frazer: *Even in his best days*
picture taken at the   *he* [Apollo] *did not always rise*
belly button of the earth?   *to verse, and in Plutarch's*
What smile is not a smile   *time the god appears to have*
of embarrassment? of   *given up the attempt in despair*
self-satisfaction? of   *and to have generally confined*
hybris? What angle of the   *himself to plain, if not lucid,*
arm does not betray a   *prose.*
certain inappropriate
possessiveness?

karpouzi:
watermelon

Only then did we realize,
we had lost our tour.

The Delphic letter E, cut into stone;
that is the mystery that no one can explain.

One day, one night, before Pausanias, before Socrates,
before Apollo (?)

the last person who knew what it means (what it meant)
perished.

That's the way it is.
The answer (or was it the question?):

ROBERT KROETSCH

                                 mislaid?
                                   stolen?
                                   revised?
                                   erased?
                                   forgotten?
                                   denied?
                                   concealed?
                                   replaced?
                                   remembered?
                                   laughed out
                                   of court?
                                   supposed
                                   to be
                                   sacrilegious?

watermelon is (not)
karpouzi

We went up the stone ramp, Laura and Meg and I. The floor, open to the sky, was as bare as a granary floor in summer before harvest begins. Six pillars remain where Croesus, told that in waging a war against a great power he would destroy a great power, heard, but did not understand.

They say that the most ancient temple of Apollo was made of laurel, and that the boughs were brought from the laurel in Tempe. The temple must have been in the shape of a shanty. The Delphians say that the second temple was made by bees out of wax and feathers, and that it was sent to the Hyperboreans by Apollo ... As to the story that they made a temple out of the fern that grows on the mountains by twining the stalks together while they were still fresh and green, I do not admit it for a moment. Touching the third temple, it is no marvel that it was made of bronze, since Acrisius made a bronze chamber for his daughter ...

The wind was a dry wind.
There might have been
no sea at all, far below,
where the Pleistos River
winds its way through the
silver-green of olive
groves, out to blue
water. The dust was a
tight and grainy dust.

Frazer: *"a golden tripod resting on a bronze serpent* etc."
A base which is believed to have supported this famous
trophy has been found by the French at the highest part of
the Sacred Way, to the east of the temple of Apollo ... The
bronze serpent on which the tripod rested is still to be
seen in the Almeidan, *the*
ancient Hippodrome, at
Constantinople, whither it
was transferred by
Constantine. The monument
consists really, not of a
single bronze serpent, but
of three such serpents so
skilfully intertwined that
their bodies appear as a
single spiral column, and
a very attentive
examination is necessary
to convince an observer
that there were actually
three serpents, not one.

after I saw Apollo's temple I
wanted to turn back; I wanted
to turn down the hill again,
down the long (the sacred)
way; it was Meg who insisted
we climb on higher: it was
her idea, there in the dust; in
the pine forest, the cicadas:
Meg said, let's climb up
higher, past the theatre (she,
pointing at the map in Laura's
book); and up we climbed,
higher, against the slope of
the mountain

"The Eggplant Poems," I
said, is a poem for which
we have no reliable text.
In fact, I haven't quite,
you might say, wrapped it
up. You mean, it doesn't
exist, Laura said. Now
wait a minute, I said. Is
there a difference between
a Greek poem which is lost
and a poem of mine which I
haven't been able to, for
whatever reasons, complete?
Yes, Laura said. Yes, Meggie said. We have references to
the lost Greek poem, I presume, Laura said, or we wouldn't
know it once existed. True, I said. True enough. But I
can tell you about "The Eggplant Poems." The eggplant, I
might add, is closely allied to the potato. Both belong to
the nightshade family. As for the poem itself ...

I had missed the moment; the voice spoke and I was not
quite ready for my own hearing. I heard only the wind.
I was tired from the climbing, dusty, trying there to follow
after my young daughters. They leapt up the steep path.

The blown dust had closed my eyes. The cicadas were loud
in the pines. The pines smelled of their own sweating.
What I heard was a smaller sound, in the wind itself,
under the pulsing rhythm of the cicadas.

(The lost poem, *Margites*.
Homer's lost, satirical
epic, that comic poem
with a fool for its hero.
That lost poem that
might have changed
the warring world.)

183

Completed Field Notes

(Sometimes,
high on a mountain,
one hears the lost poem.)

The voice reminded
me that it
had spoken. I
had heard it
there on the
temple floor while
I waited for
Meg to take
a picture. She
and Laura, together,
were studying the
(almost) vanished treasuries,
the Rock of
Sibyl. I had
noticed the olive
groves, on the
plain of Itea,
far below.

*There is a rock rising above the ground. The Delphians say
that on this rock Herophile, surnamed Sibyl, used to stand
and chant her oracles ... The earlier Sibyl belonged, I
find, to the most ancient times. She is said by the Greeks
to have been a daughter of Zeus
and Lamia, daughter of Poseidon,
and to have been the first woman
who chanted oracles; and they
say that she was named Sibyl by
the Libyans. Herophile was
younger, but still even she is
known to have been born before
the Trojan war; and she foretold
in her oracles that Helen would
grow up at Sparta to be the bane
of Asia and Europe, and that Ilium would be taken by the
Greeks on her account. The Delians remember a hymn which
she composed on Apollo ... also she says sometimes that
she is Apollo's wedded wife, sometimes that she is his sister,
or again his daughter. These poetical statements she made
under the influence of frenzy and the inspiration of the god.*

the mind
does not rhyme
with the hot wind;
         beware
any trick of
the eye.

Autobiographillyria.
That's a new word.

The cicadas in those pines. My daughters ahead of me. They had already found the stadium, the *stadion* that I had insisted was somewhere else, in my misreading of their map. They were ahead of me, farther up the mountain, out of sight.

this is what it is
to love daughters;
the cicadas sing;
the pine trees smell
of the green smell
of pine;
the tourists clamber
against the heat;
the steep trail opens
into the stone-edged
place where
horses ran

We had
passed the
temple, the
theatre too
below us;
I had
no interest
in the
stadium, the
sacred games,
the lost
sound of
colliding chariots,
the blunt
wreckage of
so many
dreams, the
bones discovering
mortality.

I was surprised at my own answer when my daughters asked me what I had asked. They knew I had fallen behind to get on with my listening. Or should I say, my questioning? They, somehow, knew that. I was surprised when I offered my explanation. I didn't have a chance, I said. My father asked the question first.

What are you doing here?
my father said.
Did I teach you nothing?

It was his awkward stating
(his farmer's patient
voice)
of the wind's ecstasy.

It was the tripod
raised to the stars.

It was the long trip
rewarded and
recalled.

It was the guidebook
lost.

The smell of blood
in the dusty air.

And the last, high
scream
of the sacrificed
beast.

Only my two daughters, smiling in their sceptical delight:
their father had heard the oracle speak. They were so
pleased with me, already I was a story to tell their friends.
We sat down on the stone seats, in the stadium. I wanted to
rest. Do you know what? they would begin, they were
already beginning, to their smiling, amused, delighted
friends. Do you know what happened ...

And I, not leading, following after my tall, blonde daughters,
there in the hot Greek sun of that August day, I had heard
the speaking in the wind.

What are you doing here?
Did I teach you nothing?

Let's miss the bus, they said, my daughters. Let's stay.
We can get back, somehow, to Athens. They wanted to stay,
there in Delphi. The small hotels around the mountain's
corner. We had noticed them. The tavernas, promising a
night of wine.

> (The poet, strayed.
> The lost poem that
> had to be lost, or
> the world with it.

> (The rippled water
> rocks the moon.

> (A penny, like the sun,
> seen from a certain angle
> surely is round.

It was I who said, We've got to go.

They wanted to stay, my two daughters. The sun came
down from the tall cliff. We had not even been inside the
museum.

It was I who said, We've got to go.

The Frankfurt *Hauptbahnhof*

I.

keep an eye peeled
for an ancestor,
me, in *das alte* country

courtesy of External Affairs,
you pay, we'll send you
the money later

me, swinging
at the old
suckerball   again

yup, well, like the guy says,
hoist (or so the story goes)
with your own peter

notation is
(what is   notation   (horse
Barrie says (in *Field Notes*)   (hero
                                      (eros
prediction,   (roses
a saying (assaying) of
what will be said: (or so
                                      (the
aerie (*prae-dic-ere*) and   (story
eagle,   (goes
both
                                      Ladies and gentlemen,
me, flying,   as you realize, we are
West Berlin to Frankfurt   in an area of turbulence.
Pan American *FLUG NR.* 641   Please remain seated.

The Frankfurt *Hauptbahnhof*

2.

Grab a cab
hustle into downtown
("the*Hauptbahnhof, please*")Frankfurt

couldn't find the train. couldn't. twenty-five parallel
and anonymous tracks. in the iron cave that is the main
station. had to catch a train to Koblenz, transfer there
and proceed to Trier. the train, couldn't find the train;
couldn't. two minutes to departure time. and the clock
running. galloping conundrum of the ricocheting sun. had
to catch the train to Koblenz:

the/ train
the train/

couldn't find the: couldn't. one minute. paralyzed.
whistlecall. and the clang-shutting of doors; on this
track, here, on that track, there, trains, to trains.
no minutes.

And when the man
came up beside me,
when he spoke
over my left shoulder,
telling me I was (I was
surprised) getting
onto the wrong train,
pointing me right, I
hardly noticed; I had
no time, even, to say
thank you   (Like the guy said.)

3.

FRANKFURT (MAIN) HBH   (the margin is a frame)
Klasse 2 EINFACHE FAHRT

von FRANKFURT (MAIN)
down the Rhine   the margin
nach KOBLENZ   is a frame of
                               (where the man
along the Mosel   spoke) silence
vineyards
to Trier

I was to give a talk (and so the story goes) on Canadian
writing to Professor Zirker's students, *Universität Trier*.
I expected to see the birthplace of one of my ancestors.
We go into the unknown, even into the unknown, with
expectations. I expected to find a *Kirche* where my
Urgrossmutter went to pray. I found a plaque marking
the birthplace of Karl Marx. I found a Roman spa that
dated back to Constantine the (280?–337) Great.

January 11, 1983:   "Great-grandmother,"
after a dish of   I shouted. "Watch out
venison and a fine   for
local wine: notation   [what happens
is a system of_____   in the margin
written down against   is what happens]
the_____.   time."

4.

on the sills of the train
windows:

Nicht hinauslehnen.   the margin
Do not lean out.   the margin

Vienna. My second day in Vienna. January 15. Schönbrunn
Palace and Park, the park dating from 1705, the palace
converted to rococo by Empress Maria Theresia (1717–1780).

I couldn't see the park for looking at the sky.

Great whirlwinds of crows. Thousands of crows, I was told
by my guide, come to the forests of this park, from Russia,
to winter. Those wintering crows. They were riding the
updrafts, thousands of crows. They rode the air up, their
wings held to soaring, those sky-proud crows; they closed
their wings to their sides and let themselves fall, corkscrewing
down at the lifting earth; they feathered out and soared
again, on the giddy laughter of their black wings.

to glance/
to gaze

                  the notation inscribed
to glance/to   by crows numerous
gaze (to gaze)   on a flighty sky:

5.

notation ➤ divination ➤ augury

in Frankfurt, when I couldn't read the schedule and find
the track my train was on. I was close to despair. I
couldn't find the train, I couldn't catch the train that
would take me to Koblenz, where I must transfer. I was,
at the time, surprised by the man's appearance. from my
left side. Like me, he was pushing a cart with his luggage
on it. he was wearing a green corduroy jacket, like mine.
he was slightly younger than I, but only slightly, a matter
of a year or two. he was shorter, but only a little. his
beard was more carefully trimmed than mine, the frames of
his glasses were of a light-coloured plastic, the sort I
should be wearing instead of metal.

as as   Double or
a concept   noting.
poses problems   My
                                doppelgänger.

as in the
example of   There in the
as ever   Frankfurt
                                Hauptbahnhof.

                                It was the crows'
                                notations that
                                told me
                                how to meet

                                the gone stranger.

6.

o the immense sadness of travel
the sadness of the smell of
                    hotel rooms
the sadness of telephone booths
the sadness of pottery for sale
                    in deserted alleys
the sadness of cameras
the sadness of folded maps
the sadness of a coffee cup on a
                    sidewalk table
the sadness of a brochure
                    that tells you
                    to go on and on
the sadness of footsteps on the
                    cobbled street outside
                    your window
the sadness of the woman in the
                    room next door, crying
                    out her relief
the sadness of timetables
the sadness of airport lounges
                    late at night
the sadness of cold candles in old
                    wine bottles
the sadness of a deck of cards
the sadness of underwear hung
                    to drip dry
the sadness of postcard stands
the sadness of the man
                    punching your ticket

(where the hell did
that margin get to)

7.

Notation is a set
of instructions for
reading (in) the
future

those sites, those ruins, as notation (o the immense sadness
of travel). the Imperial Thermae, become ruins before
completion, Constantine removing his capital to Byzantium.
a Hapsburg palace, presided over by crows. a plaque where
Marx's mother changed his diapers (and the world). and my
great-grandmother, not a trace of the old girl, and yet in
Minnesota she was famous for having shied* a stick of wood
clean across a large kitchen, through an open window, and
into direct contact with her fleeing husband's skinny ass.
and so the story goes.

*I doubt that she paused to select a verbal attitude

threw	heaved	hurled	chucked	fired	flung
cast	launched	pitched	shied	slung	sent off
released	dispatched	interrogated(?)		defenestrated	

appropriate to her

being

generally and specifically

pissed off.

8.

Notation, in *Field Notes*, Barrie, is the reader in the text.
The narrator, always, fears his/her own tyranny. The
notation in the poem occasions the dialogic response that is
the reader's articulation of his/her presence (the ecstatic
now of recognition? the longer, if not always enduring,
experience of transformational vision?).

"Silence,
please."

Bugles.

the gone stranger
the mysterious text
the necessary
transfer

the stick (or
chunk) of
wood

somehow
taking both
flight and
it would seem

aim

9.

Notation is the double of the poem. Or: we are the poem, and cannot hear except by indirection. We can only guess the poem by encountering (by being surprised by) its double. The notation announces the poem to the poem. Perhaps every poem is a poem lost (in the poet, in the reader), and can only find itself in the

broken
(the remaining)
lines

or: notation is a flying (consider the birds in autumn, e.g., a flock of blackbirds, preparing to migrate from here to there, forth and back, charging the sky electric with intent)

in order to fly: *Urgrossmutter,*
                               yes. But
                               he came out of   197
                               my body.

notes (not notation) for Jan 18. all day on a train from Vienna (Graz, actually), across Austria, into Switzerland. sharing a train compartment with one person only, an ancient woman who speaks not a word of English. we use my pocket dictionary, we point and talk, pronouncing the words hesitantly, too deliberately. she points to a mountain. she knows the names of all the mountains; she tells me their names. the skiers, abruptly, swoop down the mountains toward us. we talk our way from poetry to prose, from prose into silence.

10.

Jan 22: *Züge zum Flughafen*
      Frankfurt: Fahrplan

I was in the main railway station in Frankfurt, waiting to
take a train out to the airport. I tried to reconstruct the
occasion of my meeting with my double. I hadn't on that
first occasion been able to read the schedules and find the
track my train was on. Now, looking at the train schedules,
I found them remarkably easy to read; I was able, easily, to
reconstruct my itinerary and my actual journey.

What I could not reconstruct was the way in which I had
not been able to find my train. But the stranger had recog-
nized my confusion. He had come up beside me and had,
unbidden, spoken. He told me I was about to get onto the
wrong train. His voice at the time perplexed me, because it
was at once a foreign voice, and familiar.

How he knew where I had to get to I don't know. Perhaps
the body speaks its own destination. But the stranger who
spoke to me, the bearded man in the green corduroy jacket,
pushing his luggage on a cart as I pushed mine, had a voice
that I recognized only then, there, on my second occasion in
the Frankfurt *Hauptbahnhof*, when I was entirely alone.
Perhaps it was his hat that had deceived me on the first
occasion. He was wearing a soft cloth hat of a very conserva-
tive and yet distinguished sort. I never wear a hat—though
only a day before our encounter I had in fact, while shopping
in Berlin, attempted to buy a hat for myself. The voice of
that man who directed me onto the right train, the train
that would take me to Koblenz, where I would then transfer
onto another train and proceed to Trier, to give a talk on
Canadian writing (and I gave the talk), had been exactly my
own.

like, I   out and
mean   in and
                                out and
                                in and
                                out and
                                in and
                                out and
                                in and
                                out and
                                in and
by indirection   out and
(by indiscretion)   in and

Perhaps the bearded man in the green corduroy jacket,
pushing his luggage on a cart as I pushed mine, on seeing
me

recognized his double.

The notation   I never
keeps it moving.   wear a hat.

Sonnet #1

my first (my second) garden:
the primordial: nothingness.
Out of which.
The undomesticated.

not bad. Not bad for
a start: the garden
again, here,   north
(of) America   not

bad for a start, a snow
white page,   and this our
daily, this every: come, muse
find me my (singing): the red-winged

blackbird   by the slough
(in spring)   perched
on a dead cattail

(resist   the temptation
to give it form   resist
the temptation   )

Birthday: June 26, 1983

In the snapshot my mother is seventeen.
She is standing beside an empty chair.
Today is my birthday, I am fifty-six.
I seat myself in the empty chair

in the snapshot. My mother is standing
against the wall of a wooden house. The
wall of the house is shingled. To her
right, and behind the chair, is a window.

I am in the house, out of sight, hiding,
so that she won't remember I am not yet
born. Her waiting eyes contain my eyes.
Her mouth, almost smiling, contains mine.

The window reflects the images of the trees
that are in the yard. I am out in the yard,
playing. I am not yet her son.

In this poem I rehearse my mother.
I hold the snapshot in my hands.
I become her approaching lover.

I'm getting old now, I can tell. I dream
a lot of my mother. In my dream last night
she was in the garden, over the hill,
behind our house. She was standing. I was

playing in the pea vines. We were both happy.
Neither of us would move, in the dream. Perhaps
I wasn't playing. I was kneeling to pick peas.
My mother held in her apron the peas

we had picked together. She was standing still.
I knew she was watching me. She was
watching me grow. Like a bad weed, she liked
to say. That pleased her.

I'm getting old now. I wouldn't say I'm happy.
Serene is an adequate word. Death is not quite
the enemy it was. It is a kind of watching.

Death begins to seem a friend that one has almost
forgotten, then remembers again. In my dream,
last night, I was playing in the garden.

Sounding the Name

In this poem my mother is not dead.
The phone does not ring that October
morning of my fourteenth year.
The anonymous voice on the phone

does not say, Call Arthur to the phone.
Our hired man, a neighbour's son, quiet,
unpretentious, a man from the river hills
near our farm, does not turn from the phone,

he does not say, seeming to stress the time,
Your mother died at ten o'clock. My sister and I
do not look at each other, do not smile,
assuring each other (forever) that words are
                                        pretenders.

In this poem my mother is not dead,
she is in the kitchen, finishing the October
canning. I am helping in the kitchen.

I wash the cucumbers. My mother asks me
to go pick some dill. The ducks are migrating.
I forget to close the garden gate.

Sonnet #5

nothing

   but   .

nothing
       but
darkness
outside my
window

                           nothing
                                      but

                         darkness

                                   outside

                         my window

                         nothing but
                         darkness

the shape of
water

Sonnet for my Daughters

I think of sloughs
in early fall, the ducks
inside the darkness,
all night, talking.

In this poem my mother
stands at the window. We
listen. She names
the birds.

The birds are talking.
The phone does not ring.
There are no messages.
No one is absent.

There are mallards and
pintails, in the dark.
My mother, listening,
names their talking.

The ducks, in the sloughs,
are part of the weather.

I.

In the death of my mother
I read the empty sky.

In the death of my mother
I learn to bite the wind.

In the death of my mother
I hear the clarinet.

In the death of my mother
I say goodbye to myself.

In the death of my mother
I speak to the grass.

In the death of my mother
I enter the cave.

In the death of my mother
I recite my name.

2.

I have sought my mother
on the shores of a dozen islands.

I have sought my mother
inside the covers
of ten thousand books.

I have sought my mother
in the bars of a hundred cities.

I have sought my mother
on the head of a pin.

I have sought my mother
in the arms of younger women.

I have sought my mother
in the spaces between
the clouds.

I have sought my mother
under the typewriter keys.

3.

In the fall of snow
I hear my mother.
I know she is there.
In the weight of the snow
I hear her silence.

I count white stones
in October moonlight.

I break dry bread
with a flock of gulls.

I tear sheep's wool
from barbed wire fences.

The visible,
the visible —

where are you?

4.

These are the scars
that make us whole.

These are the scars
that empty us
into our lives.

Hold your horses.
It was a nice trip
to heaven. Let us
now visit the

earth.
The scarred earth
is our only
home.

Mother, where are you?

Envoi (To Begin With)

There is no real
world, my friends.
Why not, then,
let the stars
shine in our bones?

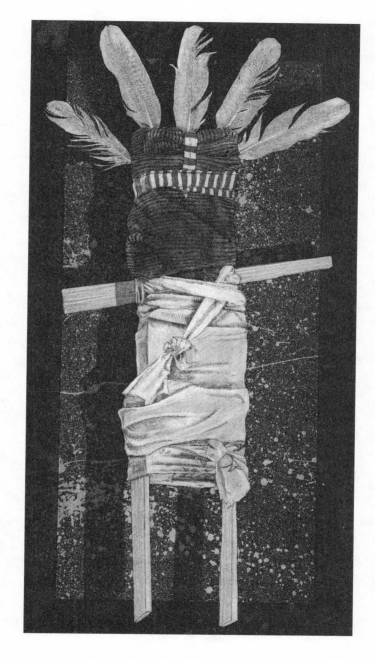

III COUNTRY & WESTERN

Excerpts from the Real World

"Perhaps if I call you forever you'll hear me toward the end."
—from *The Missing Book of Cucumbers*

Being an Introduction to Strawberries and Cream

7/1/85
I want to explain why I didn't answer the door. I knew it was you,
there. My reason for not answering was very simple at the time,
though now it seems more complex. It was late morning on a Janu-
ary day. The sun was shining blatantly.

11/1/85
You say that in your view everything is poetry. Then you go skiing
with your mother while I spend the afternoon trying to put the
scales back onto the fish.

12/1/85
Early one evening in Rome I bought four blood oranges from a
street vendor and went to my hotel room and cut each of the four
oranges in half and sat alone in my room, studying the colour of
blood oranges, listening to the rain.

14/1/85
I couldn't wear the belt you bought me to the dinner you cooked for
us in your apartment. I was wearing socks that didn't match. Your
telephone was unplugged. CBC hadn't broadcast its quota of
Beethoven for the day. The scallops were drowned in a wine sauce
that tasted of your eyes.

23/1/85

So one of us is the jealous lover. The photograph you sent me, of a strawberry on a fishhook. Thank you. I just want to explain why I sent it to you. Anonymously, of course. How did you know it was from me?

30/1/85

I have spent the entire store of my pain. My life is a portrait of the woman who deceived me into hunting the unicorn.

4/2/85

The original plan was to build a pyramid on the sand dunes of southwestern Manitoba. Blue apricots are rare. Perhaps the apricots are plums. Doors, in a manner of speaking, are descriptive. Otherwise we wouldn't be here now.

6/2/85

I should not have sought the unicorn beside the sea. Your long hair spills down your back, before we make love, like seaweed in the Bay of Fundy. When you make love. Like the Bay of Fundy.

11/2/85

Each entry, by its coming into existence, excludes itself from the potential of the poem. The spending lover both creates and fears the growing silence. Annihilation.

14/2/85

About the night we danced in the kitchen, drunk on the wine that the scallops did not drink. The socks you were wearing, you said, were your mother's. What if, for instance, we replaced the unicorn with the common mallard or the garter snake?

15/2/85

You say that, as a child, you liked playing hide-and-seek. Of the three roses I sent you, one was touched by frost. We fall through the gaps in your words. The net, too, is a container of sorts.

16/2/85

I want to explain. Words surface from inside, bringing with them vinegar and whales. Your eyes grow darker when you eat figs or when you flirt with other men. Owls pick up mice. Sky burial, you might call it.

18/2/85

Once, years ago, I was in Mexico and got sick on some lettuce I ate in a small village. Figs, on the other hand, appropriate the shade of blue that most imitates desire.

20/2/85

In the switch-blade of your tongue, the fish hawk studies mayhem. Tell me again that you love me. Which of the three roses did you put into the spaghetti?

23/2/85

Ask your friend, the mounted policeman, to read Lacan. Identity, he should realize, is at once impossible and unavoidable. Desire is that which stands outside the boundaries of satisfaction.

24/2/85

L'autre. The author. I'm not myself today. The other is a tramp. Confloozied.

25/2/85

In hopscotch, you may recall, the pieces of broken glass kiss the pavement as a beginning. And snow turns the wide world into an egg.

26/2/85

Lapwing is, improbably, the name of a bird. Titmouse. Goatsucker.

27/2/85

Our lunch in Niverville. The seed-cleaning plants were shaking the sky. You listed your truckdriver-lovers, on the paper plate, under my fish and chips. The man at the next table passed us the ketchup.

28/2/85

We are on the appropriate flyway. I have not seen a single ibis in years. The flight of butterflies, from your pubic hair, came to my nose as a metaphysical proposition. For a moment I believed in paradise.

Telegram, or, Tell Your Grandma

1/3/85

I did not intend to enter the story. It happened by accident, believe me. You were wearing sunglasses.

2/3/85

The affair I never mention, the one that turns out to be with you, was occasioned by an ice storm that toppled power lines and brought angels crashing into the frozen fields.

4/3/85

Telescopes are aphrodisiacs. The kiss you gave me last night was a comet from a galaxy which is, I now read in the almanac of your body, undiscoverable. Trucks loaded with sugar beets roar past my apartment at four in the morning.

5/3/85

Just before sunrise, I drink the juice of four blood oranges. So one of us is the jealous lover. If strawberries grew in snow, they'd be easier to find at night. I miss the smell of your hair.

8/3/85

I want to explain why I like the country & western songs you compose in your sleep. She's a cheatin lyin woman/with a cheatin lyin song./She's a cheatin lyin woman,/so I know we'll get along.

10/3/85

That role of barbed wire you put in my bed. Don't you realize I could have hurt myself, mistaking it for you?

13/3/85

Horsehair, when mixed with plaster, contributes to the durability of the wall. And, O yes, did I mention that the quality I dislike most about you is your absence? Apples are improved by the first frost. The memory is a careless optician.

14/3/85

I hadn't noticed the margin. Eli Mandel was lecturing on the myth of the frontier, this on the banks of the Oldman River, to a band of Blackfoot warriors. I fell off the page. The sun, unthinkingly (or so we assume), bruised itself on the flat horizon.

15/3/85

I liked the telegram, the one you sent me reporting my birth. And the bouquet of thistles, that too bespoke a generosity and a thoughtfulness I hadn't anticipated. But why did you have the florist send me the bill in a black envelope?

16/3/85

She was drinking straight tequila,/ she was having lots of fun./ She was laughing like a raven,/she was carrying a gun.

17/3/85

Yours are the unicorn's buttocks. I recognized that, the first time you knelt to my whisper. But how do I capture you, ever?

18/3/85

The silence of the pickerel fills Lake Winnipeg. The lake is shallow. We are building a pyramid in the middle of the lake. Once, years ago, watching a flock of ducks feeding in a slough, I fired my 12-gauge shotgun into a passing rainbow.

19/3/85

Would it not be safer for me to say, in addressing you, *Red* roses are red?

20/3/85

To live a long life. To help others. To have fun. These, the old hunter explained, are the Inuit values. This was in Eskimo Point, on Hudson Bay. A polar bear, hunting a hunter, the old hunter explained, approaches the way a cat approaches. Or something like that. He was trying to make Terry understand. My friend Terry Heath, years ago, before he visited Eskimo Point, was a collector of art.

22/3/85

Nothing pleases a perfect wife, nothing. I told that to the blizzard. The blizzard shrieked with laughter. Since then I've travelled often to strange places, rain forests and tropical islands. I'm planning a collection of turtle eggs.

23/3/85

Don Kerr invented Saskatoon by growing up inside a downtown movie palace. He refuses to record the prairie wind. Now, today, he asks for a section of my poem for *NeWest Review*. I've applied to the Canada Council for a pair of running shoes and a whistle.

24/3/85

Your nipples are the colour of pennies, found in the snow. I am a stranger's hand. Even our secrecy is become a form of devotion.

25/3/85

This is a poem I didn't write. And not because I wasn't writing.
And not because it isn't a poem. I'm beside myself, purely as a way
to anticipate the past. Endings have stems and blossoms.

On the Uncertainty of the Singer's Lamentable (_____)

1/4/85

I only buy used mirrors now. I like to see other faces when I look at
myself.

2/4/85

If it is true, as you sometimes insist, that I cannot bear to be loved,
why, then, do you, so often, transform yourself into a distant city?

3/4/85

Here on the coast of North Dakota, we pretend against our desire.
Over wine and chilled oysters, we touch each other with promises.
In the seaweed on the shore of your bed, we smell the cold film of
our spent bodies. Which of us wrote the narrative line?

4/4/85

Your body is so smooth when you sleep, lobsters, moving along the
ocean floor, bruise the water to a rougher sheen. On damp nights
especially, my tongue hides under your pubic hairs. We must be
sensible.

7/4/85

I'm delighted that you went to communion this morning. Angels,
with the loss of their natural habitat, are becoming scarcer. I'm
happy to be able to regret that I met you.

8/4/85

You are what used to be called a sharp-tongued woman. Look what
you've gone and done to my pricked rejoinder.

9/4/85
In my imagination, this morning, rabbits, coming wet out of the sea,
eat your shadow.

10/4/85
Today I'm having an affair with a wine pitcher I bought, years ago,
in Siena, and accidentally left behind in the Leonardo da Vinci
Airport, outside Rome. The radio in the kitchen is paralyzed by my
infidelity.

11/4/85
"But most of all I luv you cuz yr you." If you see what I mean.

12/4/85
I remembered you, for four days, with my broken skin. We live our
lives expecting phone calls. You dingaling.

14/4/85
Here in the Highlands the budded trees, obscenely mauve, ache to
blossom. How do man and woman, in these blocky houses, speak
against such arrays of stone? Thinking of you, I forgot to pack a
sweater. Tell your new lover to wear glass pyjamas when he sets out
from Winnipeg to transport bull semen around the world.

15/4/85
You are so far distant, I eat black pudding to keep my anger from
turning to dismay. Unexpectedly, I see that expectancy is what
draws us to the clouds, the clouds to us. Last night, late, the trees
outside my window were holding hands. I miss you, apparently.

17/4/85
When we wear wool, we wear grass. The carnivorous earth awaits
my version of reciprocity. Intertwined universes inhabit each of our
bodies.

18/4/85

Is the terrible the part we know or the part we don't? Why is it so difficult to grow apples in the dark, without having them turn into potatoes? How did the Atlantic, so dryly, assert itself between us? Did you remember to pay my hydro bill?

19/4/85

My beard needs shaping. The sun has been gone for a week. Is it possible that, for the split fraction of a second, I saw the hole in the window before the bullet pierced my skull?

20/4/85

But most of all I love you. The rabbits have no shadows of their own. The mirror falls into its own error.

21/4/85

Peter Easingwood quotes John Cowper Powys to me. "I like a chaotic anarchistic strung-along *multiverse* ..."

22/4/85

Headline in the Dundee newspaper: Corpse Found in Graveyard. To lock is to key. Even as I lay down, I heard myself walking away.

23/4/85

It was fourteen long days to the moonlight. I have won, I have won, cried the raven.

Every Idea Is a Wish

24/4/85

You live an unsigned life. Like the ashtray I bought in Edinburgh (the castle, the castle), you remind me of where I once was. Kitschy-kitschy-coo, love. And I don't even smoke. Do I?

25/4/85

Hammer Happy, the King of Babylon, sells used cars on the Pembina strip, right there in Winnipeg. Even here, now, today, this afternoon in the Yorkshire Dales, I locate my pain in the descending lines of a prairie coulee. Your heart breaks me.

26/4/85

Everything recurs (more or less). Consider, for instance, spring. Or transmission problems.

28/4/85

And so she tracked you down. You, the Shyster King of Babble On, she, with her friend Pontiac, the old chief disguised as a red coupe with mags on the rear and a four-barrelled carburetor. The three of you making it, together. Kinky.

30/4/85

"Stay gentle passenger & reade A sentence sent thee from ye dead." This I found on a church wall, in York. Ron Smith and I were shopping for Harris tweed jackets.

2/5/85

I go through the secondhand bookstores of Amsterdam, looking for a single remaining copy of my first book, the book I never wrote. It was a study of the silence of cucumbers.

3/5/85

Trying to prove that Western Canada is inscribed in Hammer Happy's six-month warranty, I watch for magpies (dancing) in the tulip fields. I try to snare gophers with a fishing line, here, below sea level.

5/5/85

Rijksmuseum. "Wild man on a unicorn with a bird. Engraving, c. 1450. From the large deck of playing cards." Self-portrait with still life. Consider, for instance, the stealth of the cucumber.

222

ROBERT KROETSCH

6/5/85

I want to explain why I mailed you that team of horses for your birthday. I know you have nowhere to keep them. Except in your mother's garage.

8/5/85

There, outside the restaurant, near the tram stop, chalked on a small blackboard: TOMAATEN EN KOMKOMMER. Every clue is, surely, a clue. *Broodje*, I tell myself, clutching at straws, must be sandwich. Bread, as a root word, belatedly, perhaps.

9/5/85

Desire, like a prairie duck, its tail feathers in the air, feeds below the surface. As Hammer Happy would have it: poet, consider shock absorbers. They are not ashamed to repeat themselves. Relax, and you'll kitsch yourself laughing.

11/5/85

And yet I felt a certain twinge of disappointment when we were told the plane was about to crash. I had intended to invest in RRSPS.

14/5/85

STASIS. Bus stop. The Greeks have a knack for starring. The un-signed hole in the universe. Not to mention the street vendors, their carts, at this time of year, heaped with strawberries. Passengers.

25/5/85

Here on Mandraki Beach, Skiathos, I undress. The wind makes of each of your nipples a cork, of my mouth a bottle that begs a signature.

27/5/85

Tsougria (Thistle) Island is presently (since The War, I'm told)
uninhabited. I squat naked beside the stone slabs of the abandoned
olive-crushing floor. I grunt and then sigh. Ah, life, I think, watch-
ing the butterflies and the lizards. I tear in half the Kleenex
snitched from your beach bag. These are the economies of islands.

30/5/85

Slices of fresh cucumber, with just a drop of vinegar, a drab of salt.
Pass me that ashtray. Let place do the signing for us. Close the
door and let me in.

The Frying Pan, and How It Was Actually Invented

7/6/85

We're on the road to Lake Winnipeg. The pelicans are measuring
the sky for a new suit of clouds. The gophers measure the width of
the road with their lives. You put your left hand on my right thigh.
Floor it, you say.

8/6/85

Two loves halve I, you wrote on your last postcard, the one you sent
from Riding Mountain. You are as beautiful as snow. I'm sorry the
hill fell off your skis.

11/6/85

They boarded up the railway station while I was inside, waiting for
the last train to nowhere. Later the same day I heard the waters of
the lake beginning to rise. Someone offered me an iron raft. Thank
you.

14/6/85

Love is a frying pan with a handle that conducts heat.

16/6/85

The sky takes on the colour of what you and I, mistakenly I'm
told, call the crocus. Why don't we, then, by way of recompense
to both Nature and Language, find a small bluff of poplars and
have a slow quickie?

17/6/85

I had no idea that, in a previous incarnation, you were a Spanish
guitarist. With a minimum of one finger, you are able to play the
music of your passionate recollection. I have come especially to like
the smell of your right hand.

18/6/85

"Harlequin Presents" Number 426. "Then he led her into the for-
ward cabin and gently laid her on the made-up berth, her fair hair
falling across the pillows. For a moment he sat on the edge of the
bunk, his eyes dark with desire as he fondled her." And besides, we
were in a rowboat.

19/6/85

Praxis makes perfect, you tell me. But I'm Daedalus on my feet.

20/6/85

Gimli Proverb. And I'll tellya another thing, young lady. If I hadn't
spent so much money on sex and booze, I'd have more money now
to spend on sex and booze.

25/6/85

We've been promised a weather of grasshoppers, yet nothing
hatches. When will you leave your retailer of bull semen, there on
the outskirts of Brandon, and buy a ticket to the Equator? In your
absence I practise sleeping in the middle of the bed.

28/6/85

And I suppose, dear, you think I have never got one of your pubic hairs stuck in *my* throat. Gates are inclined to swing both ways. Even squares are round, after a fashion.

29/6/85

We were both surprised to see the wild irises, blooming in the ditch. What is the etymology of *bush?*

5/7/85

There is, tomorrow, a 40 percent chance of showers. Even the forecasters, here in the Interlake, resort to the mathematics of doubt. I listen to my cornflakes going soggy. Somewhere, behind the sound of outboard motors, a hawk is perched on a gopher's back.

6/7/85

Your skin, after our short nap, in this hot afternoon light, tastes like Paulin's Peerless Soda Crackers. Salted, of course. Yes, it was good for me too. I had no idea you once broke horses.

You Are My Country & Western, Lullaby

11/7/85

Mr. Bad is a lady. I should have known that, I suppose. Guns are an aphrodisiac, if cowboy movies are what they seem. Last night you embraced me with all your arms. I made the mistake of counting.

12/7/85

West of Outlook, Saskatchewan, you can drive straight into the end of the world. There's a law against shade in that country. Trees are considered improper. Sometimes the cattle graze, for a whole week, in a mirage.

16/7/85

Another day of my life, washed down the gully. The camouflaged button cactus, for instance, is easily discovered by the bare foot. Barbed wire fences are not vegetarians. But then again, it's no skin off your ass, is it, love?

17/7/85

The hawk on the telephone pole, folding its wings like an angel at rest, is planning a gopher's visit to the blue sky. The grasshoppers hit our windshield like hail. You raise your head from my lap, asking what the sound is. This is called writing a landscape poem.

18/7/85

Cowboy's lament. Somebody stole my woman from me. She said his name was Mike. Or Ed. I forget which.

19/7/85

And *now* can I put on the potatoes? you say. But surely domestication is basic to the rise of civilization and the advance of the stock market. And do you mind if I take a short nap while the water boils?

20/7/85

We cherish our little sufferings, as humble as they might be. Last night it was chilly in my bedroom.

22/7/85

Does your mama know that you're going to hell?/Does your mama know that you're doing it well?/ Does your mama know how you love to screw?/She was pretty good in her day too,/they tell me.

25/7/85

When do you suppose time first began its unexpected return? The horizon is, apparently, a linguistic illusion calculated to make us feel at once secure and heroic. I am above all else happy when my tongue is in your mouth.

29/7/85

The nearest shadow was four miles away. I had only just begun that which, like falling in love, I cannot control once commenced, when a Greyhound bus, three half-tons, two galloping horses, a motorcycle gang and a woman in a convertible began to converge on the spot where I was standing with my back to the road.

30/7/85

One assumes there is some reason (as yet undiscovered) for what is called propagation. These great flocks of birds, even now, practising their migration, must be a sign. All that's missing is gin and tonic.

31/7/85

I know you'd be appalled at the idea of a faithful lover. I'll do my best.

2/8/85

Premonitions are, I would imagine, a form of hindsight. My loathing for the human species is exceeded only by my need for human companionship. That survey crew you hired, to locate the absence of desire. Has it had any luck?

3/8/85

The hawk, at least at this distance, seems to soar without moving its wings. Do your lovers dislike being staked to the ground, naked, that way?

The Dream of Leather Is Softly to Enfold

11/8/85

I remember vividly the afternoon of my childhood when, in a violent downpour that included some hail, the sky rained frogs. A few of them croaked sweetly as they fell, filling the air with rigorous prophecy. They were quite right, I can't forget you.

12/8/85

Why do shoes dream? At night I hear them, under your bed, dreaming they will carry me away to mysterious places where I'll have to learn all over again how to walk, stepping first from a slippery rock ledge onto a wet log.

13/8/85

I would like to go much deeper into the heart of breaking. We should attempt one kiss, even if one only, inside the mouth of the crocodile.

15/8/85

Here on the bullheaded prairies we praise the sun with icicles. When summer betrays us, we recover in a regimen of parkas. One winter night, in a cold frenzy, I let my tongue freeze to an iron windmill. I knew then I was destined to be your lover.

18/8/85

Style is a way of thinking. Contemplate the rodeo rider, pitched wildly about by his fancy boots.

19/8/85

And my shirts. Do they grow tired of hanging, week after week, in a closet, just on the verge of slipping off their hangers and collapsing to the floor? Does the very possibility keep my shoes awake, listening, in the dark? Why didn't you call last night?

22/8/85

Apples, my father never once said in his life, are not avocados. How can a whip crack? Lust has its complement in hurricanes and plagues. Even the cankerworm, letting itself down from the trees, is a nuisance only at the height of its cycle. What, exactly, are drumlins?

23/8/85

Stockings like yours aren't made for walking. The bathhouse by the sea, trala, is good enough, trala, for me. Or, as my father liked to remark, talk is cheap, whisky costs money.

25/8/85

The loop of the lariat takes the calf very nearly by surprise. I remember how, when I was a boy, the men, at cutting time, kept the knife clean in a raw potato. We would walk away gravely, each foot, finding itself left behind, hurrying to catch up and take the lead.

26/8/85

A goose egg, we used to call it, zero. Getting our kicks. But that was in school. We were learning. Later you would teach me naught.

28/8/85

Even elbows are easily bruised. Blood, like beer in a plastic cup at a picnic, comes in a fragile container. You say you like the glitter of spurs, raised to the shoulders of a bucking horse.

30/8/85

Water isn't afraid to fall. Wouldn't it be refreshing if, somewhere in the world, one rainbow, even if only for a moment, assumed the shape of an equilateral triangle?

31/8/85

You are a surgeon of mangos. Rhododendrons begin at home, while marigolds, given the opportunity, sport the kiss of an early frost.

1/9/85

You say that a full moon makes you hornier. If you'll pardon my grammarian's question, hornier than what? My flat-soled shoes imagine mountains.

21/9/85

Yes, I bought the tickets. I thought the sun had given up chuckwagon racing. We must get to bed early.

22/9/85

We are going to a place where things are only what they are. Or, with the barest exception, something else, but only just something else, hardly. Words are not allowed at all.

23/9/85

Dumplings are, you might say, a culinary exploration of the idea of realized chaos. I put the tickets in your purse, where you're certain not to find them.

24/9/85

The tower on the horizon was, it turns out, a beer can, dropped by someone from a speeding train. That would seem to be signally impossible, if is is at all what it is.

25/9/85

In Winnipeg the streets are skilfully designed to lead to railway tracks that can't be crossed. Poets, at the sight of an approaching train, place their poems on the tracks, hoping to have them pressed into pennies. Lovers crack sunflower seeds by placing the dried black faces of sunflowers under the wheels of locomotives that speak only to each other, from parallel roadbeds, late at night.

26/9/85

I bought two tickets, both of them for you. We are going to enter the imagination of flax. Now that winding the clock has been made unnecessary, even impossible, weavers are puzzled at how to shape their looms, and ghosts, especially those that wear black, cannot find the door of evening.

27/9/85

Words are like children skipping rope. We'll be sitting side by side.

28/9/85

I regret that I left the tickets in the top left drawer of the dresser you gave to the Salvation Army. The men who picked it up were wearing wings, which, at the time, struck me as inappropriate. In winter, in Winnipeg, the streets become maculate, iridescent, or sometimes, imitating deserts which they no longer remember, clearly visionary.

29/9/85

Caribou, for instance, know how to paw with their hoofs through snow and find silken clumps of lichen. All the flights to Hawaii, from now to Ash Wednesday, are booked by polar bears. Don't forget to bring your guitar.

30/9/85

The streets of Winnipeg, in winter, become intentional. One learns to breathe cold iron. Testicles migrate, along with snow geese and other birds of questionable courage, to bayous and estuaries. Nipples eat frozen red berries off the mountain ash and various bushes. This is a prophecy.

1/10/85

Often, while performing, you wear a blossom on your skull, and the bees that come seeking make no sound.

2/10/85

I have the tickets here in my pocket. Why I pretended to have lost them, I can't imagine. Country singers and misanthropes get to sit on the clouds. You say you love me. This must be Indian summer.

14/10/85

You are the question to all my answers. I was an echo without prior sound until you, silently, wrote, "I am counting on my fingers to remember you." If only you had got my name right.

17/10/85

Turn about is fur play. "Almost daily," you add, "I check the garden." But please, love, no fall ploughing with frost in the ground. The ploughshare, too, has its fear of the dark.

18/10/85

Hearing the day break, we pillow our heads. I want to explain. The buffalo was only there in my mind, apparently. You had forgot to set the alarm.

20/10/85

What I remember tonight is my mother at the kitchen table, cleaning eggs. The crate was not quite full. She sent me out to the barn to find one more egg. It was there, that afternoon, climbing the steps to the hayloft, I fell into the chasm between disbelief and longing.

1/11/85

The guitar plays itself on your fingers. I hear the seeds of the dandelion, torn into the air by your breath. Or is it snow I see, at the entrance to your mouth?

4/11/85

Pickerel cheeks and saskatoon pie. Those delicacies give to Lake Winnipeg at once a refulgence and a pungency. Love has its brightness too, that only the tongue can smell.

5/11/85

"When we run out of places to touch," you reminded me, "we resort to tasting." We were eating scallops. You said you have your grandmother's mouth. It was nearly midnight.

8/11/85

Don't strike a match on a rainbow. But why not?

9/11/85

There are, of course, brown cows that we refer to as red. Try putting a flame into a wooden crate marked This Side Up.

13/11/85

Years ago, playing in my bare feet on a pile of discarded lumber, I stepped on a nail. What I can't forget is not the surprise of entry but, rather, the extraction, the red-pepper grip of muscle and bone, the vacuum screaming its pain.

234

Even After We Came the Snow Was Still There, on the Roofs, Crying in the Moonlight

20/11/85

Clocks are not cuckoos, though I'm not quite certain what a cuckoo is. Comparisons are of limited use, it would seem. Your eyes, I'm told, are like precious stones. And you wonder why I'm possessive.

21/11/85

We learn to stop caring by painting the black cow white. Every passion has its colour. Why are your eyes one green, one blue? I see that you strum your guitar until your fingers begin to bleed, then you add love to your repertoire.

22/11/85

"Today I thought I saw a butterfly on a planter topped with snow." This, in your note, the one you left on the fridge, when you didn't drive me to the airport.

25/11/85

I arrived in Baghdad intending to drink yogurt and to eat fresh
dates. Even as we landed a voice on the loudspeaker system ob-
served, obscurely, "We are going down." My silence was the colour
of your pubic invitation.

26/11/85

Arabic wisdom. "The truth is too precious to share." And so our
hands grope in the dark, finding buckles and zippers. We say noth-
ing.

27/11/85

I think of ziggurats, their lifted entrances, their lost stairways. They
knew everything in advance. I had no idea the desert, from the sky,
would appear so close in colour to red.

28/11/85

Your nipples are as a pair, twinned kumquats, brazen in the sun.
But is it true they turn away, avoiding each other's light, under the
crazed umbrella of my body?

29/11/85

The festive ululations of the women, their tongues quick in the red
openess of their mouths, their voices high into ecstasy, drove me
to the bliss of ruin. I stayed in the desert forever.

30/11/85

"We live," she said, "a whole life with the same person. It makes us
very old." I sipped my coffee. From far in the distance, I heard
artillery. "Then you are not," I said, "Ishtar." She wore a dozen
bracelets on each of her golden arms. "You have known her for a
long time," she told me.

1/12/85

The bazaar is full of men who are pounding tin and copper into the roundness of your buttocks. The din of their brassy fever brought a stout handle to my hand. I watched a man turning the rim of a pan on his big toe. You poured me, softly.

2/12/85

In the dust, by the Euphrates, I put my mouth to your bum. It was right there, in bas-relief, on a brick wall the colour of sand, in the ancient sunlight. The river flows in a curve around what was once Babylon.

3/12/85

The gate is off its hinges. But I love you just the slam. And the proof of the pudding, Ishtar, is. I am mad today, with missing you. You are everywhere.

ROBERT KROETSCH

4/12/85

The date palms shape the landscape. There are two hundred varieties. Or more. Or less. How then can I call anything love, unless it is as various as you, deciduous? But leaf me be.

7/12/85

I remember clearly now. I went down onto my knees. You put your hand to the back of my neck. The water buffalo, grazing at the edge of the river, lifting its head to your long moan, looked vaguely like a unicorn.

8/12/85

Even the two ends of an egg have difficulty understanding each other. As a child I believed that rabbits lay eggs, and in that knowledge I was complete.

Spending the Morning on the Beach

Ten Related Lyrics

"We all live in the same world's sea. We cannot tell a story that leaves us outside, and when I say we, I include you. But in order to include you, I feel that I cannot spend these pages saying *I* to a second person. Therefore let us say *he*, and stand together looking at them."

—George Bowering, *Burning Water*

I can no longer keep a journal. My life erases everything I write.

Fiji

Realizing the poem for him has lost its expectancy, he heads directly for Fiji. He flies by Air New Zealand, out of L.A. Nadi is dark to his landing.

The Southern Cross signals the upset world. Even westward is lost in east. We are not where we were.

This island's murder was for sandalwood. The European trader and the Chinese aesthete drank tea together without shame. Any aesthetic has a terrible will. He registers at the Sandalwood Inn.

Waiting for the dining-room to open, he hikes down to the beach. The parrots in the coconut palms are noisy in the sunrise.

Somewhere in his recent flying is a lost day. Words are like that. Once upon a time he was a gardener of the possible fruition.

Here in Fiji he drinks the juice of passion fruit, he eats papaya and a thin slice of fresh pineapple for breakfast.

Brisbane

There is salt on his skin.

Realizing he's no longer obliged by the ache in his body to write poems, he watches the grasstrees burning free of their dead leaves. The squat black trunks exhaling wisps of smoke wear each and fashionably a tassle of green hair. All this, just as he'd begun to hope for a vision of hell. At lunch, for instance, he's joined by a pair of kookaburras, hopping down from a gum tree onto the balcony of the Griffith University Club. We come to conclusions. He calls to mind Odysseus, somewhere on a beach, hiding his nakedness yet keeping it available. The skinks loll in the sun, the possum sleeps toward an awakening of darkness.

There is salt in the fluids of his body.

He has the whole day.

Noosa Heads 1

On the way up to Noosa Heads he stops in a cloud of gum trees to visit an avocado farm. The avocado trees, in eight varieties, drip avocados into a sequence of harvest times. He breaks in two a custard apple. The seeds are covered in a white substance that is almost slimy, yet sweet to the tongue. He climbs a road to a banana plantation, the fruit growing ripe in blue plastic bags high on the tall plants. After fruiting the plant dies.

He goes with Doug into Noosa National Park. They are two poets on vacation. But what do poets take vacations from? What, ever, is the possibility of other? They hike into the native forest. They find the nude beach, Alexandria, and take off their clothes and lie on the sand.

Realizing the poem is the tormentor of his sleep, he strangles it by his refusal, in the hot sunlight, to close his eyes. Each surfer is a small miracle of stillness and motion. Each surfer slips down a rising wave, then disappears into a bed of foam.

Doug tries bodysurfing. He engages the windmill of his own recklessness. The sun recovers him.

Noosa Heads 2

> 20 May 86
> sunrise 6:23
> sunset 5:05

Realizing *poetry* is a mousetrap on the tongue, he calls ashore for water.

He is somewhere under the failed wave. The sand scours his eyes. He hardly bothers to hold his breath.

The self-portrait is a found object, signed by yours truly, as we all know. Climbing the dunes behind the beach, he finds the shade of a tree.

It is Doug, alone on the beach, who learns the semiotics of nakedness. It's a matter of spacing, Doug says.

It's a matter of knowing when to look and when not to look.

The mathematics of the gaze: angle and tangent and the theory of the line.

The self-portrait is a found object, given a name by another, appropriated. The slide (the sly) of metonymy.

It is early winter, a morning in May.

Geelong, Victoria

Realizing the poem. Talking the poem onto the page or
writing the poem onto the tongue. Realizing he cannot foil
his own inertia, he steals a pomegranate.

The fruit in Brian's garden: fig, lemon, peach,
pomegranate, pear, apricot, lime, apple, kiwi, passion fruit
and feijoa. Not atoll, says the cockatoo.

Brian foretells the future by riding a surfboard along the
edge of a hurricane. Even now, the Solomon Islands lie in
devastation.

At the waterfront they find a fishing boat unloading its
morning catch. A Vietnamese man and woman, elderly, are
dickering for snapper. One of the fishermen rinses two
fish over the side of the boat, then fillets them on the deck.

Dropping the bones back into the water.

Spitting out the seeds, into the water, is half the fun.

Sydney

Realizing that light, not dark, is the poet's affliction, he
gives himself the Governor General's Award For Not
Writing Poetry for the year 1999.

He leaves his hotel in Kings Cross and goes to see the art
show, ORIGINS ORIGINALITY + BEYOND, the Biennale of
Sydney 1986.

He stops first at the Art Gallery of New South Wales,
then buys a map and finds his way to Pier 2/3, on Walsh
Bay, where the larger works are on display in an old pier
building.

Magdalena Abakanowicz, SEVEN STANDING FIGURES
Robert Adrian, 76 AIRPLANES
Julie Brown-Rrap, BREAK AND ENTER—EXHIBITS 1–4

Braco Dimitrijevíc, MEMORIES OF COLUMBUS, FRIEND
Richard Killeen, TIME TO CHANGE THE GREEK HERO
Wolfgang Laib, THE SIXTY-THREE RICE MEALS FOR A STONE

Vivienne Shark Lewitt, LAST NIGHT I WENT TO
                                        MANDALAY AGAIN
Rainer Mang, DEUTSCHER MANN SUCHT WAS
Carlo Maria Mariani, GUARDASI IN UNO SPECCHIO CELESTE
            (LOOKING AT ONESELF IN A HEAVENLY MIRROR)

Marta Minujin, THE BOOK'S PARTHENON
Luigi Ontani, YOUNG MAN WITH FRUITS
Therese Oulton, MORTAL COIL

Yumiko Sugano, WHALE'S GENERATION
Masami Teraoka, HANAUMA BAY SERIES/CAMERA CREW
                                AND BLOWHOLE I   241

Michael Nelson Tjakamarra, POSSUM DREAMING

Anon, Canada, 1927, SELF-PORTRAIT OF POET or
                        THROWING IN THE TOWEL, EH?

Completed Field Notes

Wellington, New Zealand

Realizing he is done with poetry, he goes to a museum to
see a reconstruction of an extinct New Zealand bird, a bird
that was flightless, huge, possibly the largest bird (height
to 12 feet) that ever lived, the Giant Moa. Now how's that
for self-pity?

The poem as quotation:

> Merino Sheep: The oldest and most numerous breed
> in the world. Originated in Spain or North Africa.
> First sheep in N.Z. Captain Cook brought four in
> 1773, they did not survive. Wool: fine fibre, used in
> quality woollen and worsted fabrics.

> Feel free to stroke Lindale's stock through the fence.

> Murray Grey Cattle: This breed came about by
> accident when in 1902 a Shorthorn cow was crossed
> with a black Angus bull, the result a grey calf, a
> Mulberry. This unwanted cow survived to produce 12
> Mulberries. The name change came in the 1960s. Very
> adaptable, the breed has prospered in N.Z. conditions

> Sheep and cattle may nibble for nuts but will not bite.

The poem as evasion.
The poem as resignation.
The poem as a net
that drowns fish.
The poem as a postcard
sent directly to the sun.
The poem as POET TREE.

Rotorua

Realizing that poetry is a hospital for the sane, he watches
the Maoris building their replica village.

The thermal reserve, Whakarewarewa. A volcano's dream
of a poem. Pohutu Geyser, as unpredictable as love. The
mud pools bubble and pop, under the twisting steam. The
forest tries to untie itself.

He cannot take the light in his hands. Pumice and sulphur.
If the volcano's crater becomes a lake. If the beach itself is
beached, high and dry.

Orpheus, nothing, says the parakeet.

Orifice.

If the carved boat floats in a sheltered pool, and the iconic face bites its defiant tongue, then we have come to see the picture.

North of Auckland, Parry Kauri Park

They are in the park. The sign at the gate says the park will be locked at 5 P.M. It is 5:05. The park is locked.

The larger of the two kauri trees is eight centuries old.

The second tree, only 25 feet in girth, is younger by two centuries. The flock of rosellas inhabits the crown of the older tree.

Or are those birds, more exactly, red-crowned parakeets? He lifts the lenses of his glasses against the drift of rain. The rain lifts the coastline into these hills.

He and Steve climb out of the half-ton just as the old woman appears from her cottage door, makes a smart right turn, begins her approach.

(It was earlier in the morning. The paddock was all steep hillside. Steve ordered the dog to bring in the cattle. The dog in one easy leap cleared the high fence.)

You didn't read the sign, did you? the old woman says, at once patient and yet a bit testy.

It looks that way, he tells her. I realize that.

The Hibiscus Coast

Realizing the poem is a cruising shark, he curls his toes in the mud.

The horses train softly on the hard sand. He drops his camera into a mangrove swamp. He believes it was an accident. The man in the shed by the mangroves is building a boat.

There are sharks in these waters, the Maori farmer says, but not so many as on land. His wife goes into the paddock to feed her horses and latches the gate.

Hibiscus. Herbs, shrubs or small trees of the mallow family. With dentate leaves and large showy flowers. They grow around the gas stations, even. And in the parking lots.

Sighting two dolphins, just out from shore, rising and gracefully diving, he hurries into the water.

1.

Periodic fits of paradise exhaust him.

For instance. There is, he either knows or imagines,
in the midst of her body a tropical island.

For instance. He sits on a bench in Old Market Square,
his bottle of sugary wine concealed in a Gucci bag.

He cannot decide which text to take with him on the
long read, and therefore consults the patterned flight
of her painted toenails.

He is trying to pretend he didn't receive her letter.

Each time he takes a drink he watches with his tongue
for a message.

2.

Honeyman, she say, you ain't nothing but a phase of
the moon. And you is *waning*.

Even if words are words, and they well might be.

Even if after precedes before, and in a way it must.

The Nairn Overpass has been under repair since before
it was completed. Railway engineers, passing beneath
its uncertain arch, speak wisely of the decline of
empires. One of the winos who sleeps in its shade
has added a sundeck to his shopping bags.

The horses, every Sunday morning at Assiniboia Downs,
draw straws to see who will lose.

I guess this is par for the course.

3.

A speedboat walks on the water just down from the dock
by the Grey Nuns' cemetery.

The elm trees put on collars of glue for visiting
caterpillars.

Somewhere a fiddler is trying to catch a moth that
has gotten into his fingers.

The fish in the aquarium in a Chinese restaurant just
off King Street have ordered Shrimp with Black Bean
and Garlic Sauce (No. 83) for dinner.

What if a tidal wave sweeps up from Lake Winnipeg and
drowns all the cats?

I didn't mean to change. But he did.

4.

The sun puts in its tongue at our window.

Your hands are the feast of my body. My skin devours
the gentleness of your fingertips.

It was a night during Folklorama. He had sampled the
national foods of thirty-one nations. I'm not myself
tonight, he said.

Even Portage Avenue, last winter, was heaved in places
by frost, and lesser streets shivered for weeks in
long white mittens that looked vaguely like pillows.

Your fingers graze on my belly.

Peephole will say we're in love.

    5.

Basements all over the city are glum with summer rain.

The pelted flowers hold conferences on the lee side
of backyard fences.

A crew of men in rubber boots, waving shovels at every
passing cloud, tries to open a sewer main on Waverley.

Drifting paddleboats on the Red claim to be arks and
offer a night of music and romance to all drowning
lovers who come in pairs.

Sometimes a clap of thunder is so loud the new conductor
of the Winnipeg Symphony gets out of bed to take a
bow.

Ka-choo! I whispered, softly, in your right ear.

    6.

How do you suppose butter was discovered? Imagine
that moment,

that first, hesitating motion of the finger past the
lips,

the questioning face, the butter on the tongue,

the slow flood of radiance.

When he saw you, there on the corner of Portage by
The Bay, waiting for the light to turn green, your
arm draped over the unicorn's back,

he melted.

7.

On the first morning of the year 2000,

I told you I had won two free rides to the moon. I
trust you can use them.

Both teams scored at exactly the same time. The
computer screen over centre-ice, much to the delight
of the assembled spectators, recorded the ecstasy as
a pair of interchangeable numbers.

In Polo Park the shoppers wear winged shoes. Their
eyes are starlit probes, their fingers nibble at sixty
new objects in any given hour. The day is a surfeit
of visual dreams.

I thought I had a story you were going to tell.

Somewhere, in the far distance, a siren whispers its
feverish response.

8.

The farmers around the city burn stubble and straw.
The drifted smoke wraps our bodies in memories of
dissolution.

The lean flames wear the night/
thin with their hunger.

In my reaching to find you I find I am not yet born.

My recollection is only of what must be. The city
drifts in amniotic smoke. The sky is a membrane darker
than earth.

Your fingers smell of cucumbers. Of vinegar. Of
freshly chopped onions.

Your fingers fall on my body like rain.

9.

I AM/naught. That's all I is.   Mmmmmmmmmmm.

Zzzzzzzzzzzzzzzzz.

The first time our mouths opened and our tongues ran
hot and wet in their impossible wish to exchange places
( )

The first time the voice said huh-uh—

Even the snow is falling. The 727 coming in low across
the Assiniboine snores its way clean through the
mayor's bedroom.

Even good things have to end, his mother said. This
was at his birth.

10.

The fear of

            paradise

haunts all our
dreams.

I'm sorry,
I said, I thought

I wanted
            (you)

to be happy.

ROBERT KROETSCH Author's Note

The poems in this collection appeared over a period of fifteen years, beginning in 1973. "Stone Hammer Poem" turned out, against my own anticipation, to be prologue to a series of related poems. I did not recognize until I heard the dialogue of "Seed Catalogue" with "The Ledger" that I had in effect commenced a series of related poems that would in devious ways seek out the forms sufficient to the project (I leave it nameless) announced by Wordsworth and Whitman and rendered impossible by the history and thought and art of the twentieth century. Since the eloquence of failure may be the only eloquence remaining in this our time, I let these poems stand as the enunciation of how I came to a poet's silence. And I like to believe that the sequence of poems, announced in medias res as continuing, is, in its acceptance of its own impossibilities, completed. What I offer below is a minimal account of the text's own elaboration of its mystery and its determination.

251

"Stone Hammer Poem" first appeared in an anthology of new work, *Creation* (Toronto: New Press, 1973), and was reprinted in my *Stone Hammer Poems* (Lantzville, B.C.: Oolichan Books, 1975). "The Ledger" first appeared in *Applegarth's Follies*, Volume 1, Number 1, out of London, Ontario (1973), and was published as a book by the editors of that journal in 1975. Once the sequence had clarified itself (and notions of clarification are based on hindsight) the books appeared as follows: *Seed Catalogue* (Winnipeg: Turnstone Press, 1977); *The Sad Phoenician* (Toronto: Coach House Press, 1979); *The Criminal Intensities of Love as Paradise* (Lantzville, B.C.: Oolichan Books, 1981); *Field Notes* (Toronto: General Publishing, 1981); *Letters to Salonika* (Toronto: Grand Union Press, 1983); *Advice to My Friends* (Toronto: Stoddart, 1985); *Excerpts from the Real World* (Lantzville, B.C.: Oolichan Books, 1986). "Spending the Morning on the Beach" appeared in a new edition of *Seed Catalogue* (Winnipeg: Turnstone Press, 1986). "After Paradise" appeared in the Winter 1987 issue of the literary journal, *Prairie Fire*. The first edition of *Completed Field Notes* was published by McClelland and Stewart, Toronto, in 1989.

I wish to thank the people associated with the University of Alberta Press—Glenn Rollans (past director), Jonathan Hart, Cathie Crooks, Chris Wangler, Alan Brownoff and Leslie Vermeer—for bringing this volume into a new century in so handsome a form. The book itself speaks the details of their contributions. I wish to thank Fred Wah for the illuminations of his Introduction. And finally I want to thank the readers who, by their generous strategies, make these poems a continuing sequence after all.